TRIP 1964

TRIP 1964:
IN WHICH A CYCLING TRIP TO ROME IS RESURRECTED
Leon van Schaik and John Turner

## CONTENTS

| | |
|---|---|
| 7 | Preamble |
| 11 | John's Introduction |
| 21 | Leon's Introduction |
| 31 | Timeline Part 1 – BELGIUM/NETHERLANDS |
| 37–115 | Day 1–26 |
| 117 | Timeline Part 2 – NETHERLANDS/GERMANY/AUSTRIA |
| 121–191 | Day 27–52 |
| 193 | Timeline Part 3 – ITALY |
| 197–337 | Day 53–end |
| | Reflections |
| 341 | John |
| 363 | Leon |
| 371 | Bibliography |
| 373 | Index |
| 379 | Acknowledgements |

Cloisters and garden at the centre of Borlase School, the school where John and Leon first met and formed their friendship (JT's uncle)

PREAMBLE

1964, Spring. Two young men, John Turner and Leon van Schaik, school friends, still in their teens, set off from England to cycle to Rome, their "Trip64". Leon wrote a daily journal, John drew and photographed. That journal structures this account, and the timelines are derived from it. Leon's first Trip64 night on 6 May (Day 1) was spent in Ostend Youth Hostel and John's first night on 27 May (Day 22) was under canvas in a field close to Maassluis. They met up on 31 May (Day 26) in Amsterdam and remained together until arriving back in England in early August. When the trip ended, they were home in Buckinghamshire, preparing for university. An unremarkable 'gap-year' activity you might think, yet that journey cut through a world barely recognisable today. The Second World War still formed a bell jar over everything, colouring our perceptions. Even in the early 1970s the wearing of a leather coat evoked sinister associations. The Iron Curtain hung across Europe, limiting the horizon. A veil of fascism hung over Spain and was soon to occlude Greece. 1984 lay in the unimaginably distant future. The Campaign for Nuclear Disarmament was mounting its marches from Aldermaston to Trafalgar Square. The lives of adults were framed by reconstruction. Although British Prime Minister Harold Macmillan had announced "you've never had it so good" on 20 July 1957, the full force of the post war economy lay ahead, and Jean Baudrillard's book 'The Consumer Society' was to be published in 1970. Cars did not yet dominate roads. In England, traffic jams hardly happened except in The New Forest on August Bank Holiday. Travel was an adventure for the young, and a 1957 book explaining how to do 'Europe on Five Dollars a Day' when six dollars equalled 20 shillings seemed targeted on wealthy Americans. That many shillings would last a week, as the soon to be students would discover. And most alien to how we live now, life was lived in analogue. The internet lay fifty years ahead. The boys had planned their journey in advance, plotting routes using a guide to the location of Youth Hostels, and having no guarantee that there would be a place in one until they arrived and knocked on the door. Contact with home was by post to a few pre-planned collection sites. Each photograph taken had to be carefully considered as film was so expensive. The past is a different world.

We, the septuagenarians that those young men now are, have been haunted by vivid memories of how things were, when we were there. That is why we have now marshalled and cross-referenced the journal written by one of the cyclers, the

photos, surviving artefacts and drawings of both, into as accurate a recollection as we can conjure. Framed by independent introductions and concluding reflections, a three-part timeline for the trip structures the material. Part 1 documents solo journeys through the lowlands and concludes with our meeting in Amsterdam. Part 2 covers the journey to Venice; Part 3 carries through to Rome. There are mysteries. Some days seem to have gone missing. No amount of trawling resurrects a shared account of the journey home from Rome. Maybe that is apt for what was a pilgrimage through a little of west European culture, a journey towards adulthood, spiritual only in that sense. Even then, the weight of the future pressed on what was said and recorded. We were 'such stuff as dreams are made on', and our 'little lives'[1] beckoned. There are delights here. See for yourself!

1   The last lines of Shakespeare's The Tempest.

John's father's canoe trip to the Moselle in 1937 - 27 years later John and Leon spent the night by the confluence of this river with the Rhine (JT's father)

## JOHN'S INTRODUCTION

What lay behind my undertaking the cycling trip to Rome that this book records? Just as my love of my family and friends impels this account, my family history, my parents' encouragement for me to be adventurous, push barriers and to step into the unknown, my childhood, my schooling, my friendships, all played a part.

My father's teenage years were spent living on his parents' nursery in St Leonards, Sussex where, when not at school, he enjoyed the outside world, the seaside and winning swimming trophies. When the family moved close to the Thames in London he got into canoeing. With his canoeing club he travelled to various locations, including the river Moselle in Germany. Leon and I were not far from this location in the summer of '64, my father there in the summer of '37. WW2 started in Sept '39 so it was not surprising, in view of the British pennant on my father's canoe, that the odd pot shot was fired generally in his direction from the banks.

Before WW2 my father, an aeronautical engineer, worked for South American Airlines at London Heathrow airport. He moved at the outbreak of WW2 to work during the day in a company on the Slough Trading Estate, Slough, Buckinghamshire, making parts for the Spitfire fighter (my favourite thing visually that man has ever made). At night he either sat on the Ack-Ack gun behind the Trading Estate to fire at German things in the sky or patrolled the Thames near Maidenhead, Berkshire searching with a wooden rifle for German mini-submarines in the water. My father clearly passed on his single mindedness to me.

Soon after the war when I was 2, my parents decided to move into the country to Seymour Plain near Marlow, Buckinghamshire to bring up their children. I was encouraged to find my own fun unaccompanied, which could by some be seen as benign neglect, as soon as I was able – building dens, climbing tall trees, cycling miles up hill and down dale, and even visiting "conscientious objectors" who had seen out the war in weird buildings behind our house. When not doing all this I helped to feed and collect eggs from the 100 chickens, 40 ducks and 12 geese we had, as well as help with the 3 goats, all part of the self-sufficient world my parents wanted in those post-war days. I was also put to work in the veg plot. At the start of primary school, it was made clear I had to find my own way down to Marlow and back.

Looking back on my early life, it is easy to see now how my interests in the man-made environment, making things and the physical realities of the world, primed me for the direction

my life would eventually take. A few memories are still vividly with me.

- Digging holes in the ground to build a below ground but roofed space of my own, discovering how the earth changes in its composition dependent on depth, how animals and insects also live underground, trees, plants and streams have quite big bits in the ground and how rain can easily fill your underground home.
- Climbing tall trees made me realise they were very clever things that put branches in the right place to climb up, provide supports to build a space of my own out of reach above the ground and to cut off a branch often made the tree lean to one side.
- When you fell out of tall trees, bushes helped you not to hit the ground too hard.
- Jumping off the roof of a barn using umbrellas did not stop you from hitting the ground very hard.
- The wonders of my father's workshop, with its tools and materials just made my toes curl every time I went in there. I always wanted to make something, and if only two bits of wood were lying about I would fix them together.
- On my solitary walks to and from school down in Marlow I noticed rainwater on the road was caught by small trenches running away from the road to bigger ditches and how it was possible to vary this flow by messing about with things.
- At school we were told to cross our ankles when sitting at our desks.
- When it was getting dark, why did a switch make more light at school but at home a match was needed?

It was only later in life that I learnt about geology, structural design, drainage, velocity, central heating, engineering services (including that electric lighting installations could be turned on just by throwing a switch but that gas lighting installations needed the gas to be lit automatically or by a match at each light fitting) and the like, all of which had had their seeds planted in my young mind.

My father's own example and encouragement for me to be adventurous, push barriers and to step into the unknown, just like he had done when he was young, had led me into camping and boating trips at an age most parents would have insisted on coming along. Later as a teenager these were followed by two hitchhiking journeys around western Europe with a school pal. My upbringing really did set me up for my future life in terms of determination and outward confidence. Although inwardly I often felt unconfident, as I still often do now, my

Borlase School's 1962-63 1st VIII rowing crew and coaches taken in the cloisters garden (M W Keen, High Wycombe)

determination made me into an apparently confident person as it turns something negative into something positive. It was in 1957, when I had reached the age of 11, that Sir William Borlase's School in Marlow took over the batten of developing these parts of my character, although for me not by classroom work but by sport. Immediately behind the school is a good old Chilterns hill full of chalk and flints. This part of the hill had been cut out to make the main rugby pitch, called the Home Meadow, creating a high bank at the end furthest from the school. There was a tradition, when I entered the school, of older boys throwing the new arrivals down this bank – I physically fought off such an indignity and Leon arrived not as a first former.

I never really liked any school as such because it took me away from enjoying things I preferred to spend my time doing. The only "classroom" subjects I really enjoyed were art and physics.

Throughout my days at Borlase I relished the art lesson run by Robin Pitman in the first floor newly built art room. Robin's ability to open up boys' minds to the pleasures of drawing and sculpting was noticed elsewhere, with an edition of the BBC's Monitor arts programme featuring his work. I had always enjoyed painting and drawing, but not until my Borlase days did I receive any real instruction and direction to improve and develop, which in turn brought satisfaction. Physics I took to wholeheartedly, because it seemed to be an extension to my activities ever since I had moved to Seymour Plain all those years ago. It was logical and understandable unlike the often-twinned subject in schools of chemistry that, to me was gobbledygook and smelly (in the chem lab anyway). My 6th form subjects chosen for me were all sciences (including chemistry) and no arts. I was not happy with this. It almost took a re-writing of the school's standing orders to allow me to study maths, physics, and art A-levels (dropping smelly chemistry), but only after one of the two years in the sixth form had passed by. Only my last full school year contained the things my early years had laid foundations for.

The sports I excelled in were running, rugby and rowing (my 3R's), representing Borlase against other schools in all of them until I chose to drop running and then rugby to concentrate on rowing. However, rugby was my preferred sport initially because to be able to row one had to have passed through puberty. At rugby I played in the first Borlase team at each age up the school, often on the Home Meadow which was unlike the lush Colonel's Meadow Leon talks about. It was real character building – due to the flints in the pitch there could not have been a single match when the two teams

(above) Borlase 1st VIII launching their boat at the Rowing Club close to Marlow bridge (JT's father)
(below) Preparing to row up stream to race a Borlase Old Boys crew (JT's father)

did not retire to the showers on the final whistle without some bloody wound or other. I was selected for the Bucks, Berks and Oxon counties team but stopped when I reached 15, prior to a potential U16's call up, because rowing had by then developed different muscles within me which made me slower across land.

It was in '62 and '63 that I dropped my camping and boating trips and undertook long distance hitchhiking trips in the summer holidays through France or Germany, always with Italy as the final destination. In those days hitchhiking was normal and accepted and not dangerous like it is today. However, after these trips I decided that rather than standing in uninteresting places outside towns or on approach roads to major routes, only seeing lots of tarmac and the insides of vehicles and little else between major centres, I would rather choose a slower all-seeing mode of travel.

It was in the Art Room and the Rowing Club that Leon and I started to build our friendship. Leon was so different from my other friends I had at the time – broader thinking, interested in things that spanned both the arts and sciences, completely different early years to what I had experienced and perhaps the first "foreigner" I had got to know well. Those days spent at his family's house between Bourne End and Cookham were great – his architect father working in a back room over a weekend while his pretty mother cooked us lovely meals I had never eaten before, and then the walk to a pub in Cookham to have an evening of beer and to do sketching before my haul back home to Flackwell Heath. All of this and my previous hitchhiking journeys to Italy in my mind, gave rise to the idea of a cycle trip to Italy and Trip64 was born.

During my time at Borlase, at the end of 1st year a selection was made by the school to divide the two-form intake into Form 2A or Form 3B for the next academic year based on 1st year performances. If you went into the "B" stream, strangely the one for brighter boys, you took A-levels in your 5th year, thereby having a second go at them in your 6th year to try for better grades if you needed them. By some miracle I went into the "B" stream and, I assume, also Leon when he started at the school in 1960. On the basis of the first go at A-levels we both got university interviews followed by offers in late 1963. My interview is still in my mind. I arrived at Sheffield Midland station in my school uniform, went outside to find a bus to the university and was shocked by a huge advertising board which said words to the effect that "Only real men drink Tetley's" – did this mean Sheffield was teetotal? At the time I only knew Tetley tea. I found the bus and the conductor looked me up and down and said, in what I

John exhibiting his bike (with kit mounted) to his father at home in Flackwell Heath shortly before John departed to meet up with Leon in Amsterdam (JT's father)

later knew as a Sheffield accent, "university lov?" The conductor pushed me off the bus at the right place and a passer-by directed me to a church hall where I was interviewed in a room off a first-floor gallery and then shown the 1st year "studio" below full of hungry looking people. I went home bemused, but when the offer arrived I accepted and cancelled other applications ... Trip64 was on!

Now to earn money for the trip. I thought of returning to the bra-packing job I had done on Saturdays in recent years. But, instead, I left that to Leon and got a job where my father worked, and I had also worked before – it was the Spitfire component manufacturing company my father had worked in during the war! It was in a different building and there were no Spitfires to build but it was reasonable money for hammering part numbers on aircraft components alongside a welcoming group of middle-aged ladies. With additional funds from my mother and father I was ready for the off by the middle of May 64. During this time Leon's father helped us to plan our route to ensure we saw modern buildings as well as old. Overall though we only "sort of" planned our route. We knew we would be starting in Holland, with Leon going ahead of me to visit where his ancestors came from, would then meet up in Amsterdam, would enjoy the Rhine, would drink in the Hofbräuhaus in Munich, would go to Salzburg to stay a few days with relatives of Leon's and definitely spend time in Venice, Florence and Rome. For the bits in between we would have just read the maps we had, checked where Youth Hostels were and probably road heights above sea level to avoid too many massive climbs. Sounds like irresponsible teenagers to me! I stripped down my bike, rebuilt and checked it as much as I could afford, including removing the derailleur gear mechanism because I was not confident enough my original bike building from scratch would see me to Italy, and prepared myself for the unknown.

Leon, (arms akimbo left) and John (arms akimbo right) chatting after racing the Borlase Old Boys crew (JT's father)

## LEON'S INTRODUCTION

In 1964, two youths in their late teens, intent on careers in architecture and the arts made a cycling trip from London to Rome, discovering much about the world that they would live in and a little about themselves.

Trip64 for me is a chronicle of adolescent awareness. Physicist Carlo Rovelli writes in Helgoland (Allen Lane 2021), p 41: Adolescence is the time when the networks of neurons in the brain suddenly rearrange themselves. Everything seems intense, everything is alluring, everything is disorientating.

This intensity is, I think, why the adults these youngsters became are still haunted by the relatively short journey that they undertook. While the young men were born towards the end of the second world war, they grew up in its shadows. This was a general condition. For example, at Harvard in 1966, fully two years after our trip, David Forrester recalls attending a seminar with Henry Kissinger and Stanley Hoffman. The topic: 'Post-war Europe.' (LRB Vol 43 No 1, 31 Jan 2021). In 1964 the shape of the future was far from evident. Everything we saw spoke of its past, and simultaneously of a nascent present. Our futures beckoned.

How did these young men come to know each other? In the autumn term of 1960, aged 15, turning 16 on the 25th of October, Leon commenced study at Sir William Borlase's School in Marlow, Buckinghamshire, where John was already a pupil. Leon's parents, Gwen Greene and Johan van Schaik, active members of the South African Liberal Party with its slogan of "One man, one vote, irrespective of race colour or creed', had been made economic migrants by the South African government and opted to start life again in England. Canada had been the other option, but Johan was a life-long anglophile and Gwen had fond memories of England. They chose the Thames Valley because during her early childhood Gwen had spent time with her mother's family in Twyford, where the family were millers. Borlase was chosen for me because my mother's great uncles had been to school there, reporting that they were given ale to drink at breakfast. Johan, who worked in Marylebone in London rented the gate lodge to Hedsor House high above Taplow, the station from which he commuted, and later a thatched house on the Riversdale estate between Cookham and Bourne End.

Borlase had a certain romance to it. Founded as a charity aimed at educating the young men of the district, as were so many old schools, it was endowed in 1624 by local MP Sir William Borlase (c1564–1629) in memory of his son Henry, MP for Aylesbury, who died in that year. The Borlase family, who

were Normans, took their name from an estate near Penzance. William lived at Bockmer near the once lovely Thameside Village of Marlow, which still had forty public houses when we were at school there. Newly appointed school prefects had to run the gauntlet of these drinking places. I think I managed five! Adjacent to the school's mostly 19th century knapped flint and brick quoined bulk was a picturesque cottage, once lived in by Percy Bysshe Shelley. Opposite this and facing the school cricket ground was a red brick mansion, approved of by Sir Nikolaus Pevsner in his Buildings of Buckinghamshire. The cricket pitch was notoriously unmanageable, swelling unaccountably in certain weathers. The story was that a Cavalry Colonel who had served under Wellington lived here and when his horse died, he buried it in the field that later became our cricket ground.

Marlow was famous for its diminutive chain-link suspension bridge, the chains suspended from two elegant triumphal arches through which vehicles could pass one at a time. This was the quarter scale model of the bridge subsequently built between Buda and Pest, the elegance surviving the upscaling magnificently.

At Borlase it was eagerly expected by the sports master that Leon would join the rugby team, but knowing his ineptitude in that game, Leon opted to join the rowers, and thus was thrown into the company of John Turner. Over three school years during which they took their 'O' and 'A' level exams and Leon took an 'S' level that won him a place at Cambridge, a firm friendship grew between them. As oarsmen we were in the Borlase 1st Eight for our two last school years. A highlight was winning our class in a borrowed clinker eight when our new shell, while being transported to Reading, was snapped in two on a hairpin bend on the Berkshire cliffs of the Thames, opposite Marlow. Perhaps our most wonderful rowing experience was after losing our second heat at Henley Regatta, and having downed a pint, the eight we were part of gently and harmoniously rowed our shell back from Henley to the boatshed adjacent to Marlow Bridge. In my memory we drifted through a long summer evening passing through the shadows of trees and floating on sparkling ripples of reflection of the low sunlight. During our last outing in the end of season Staines Regatta, we were nearly swamped by pleasure boat wash, and my last memory is of my diminutive ninety-year-old Great Aunt Dora in a black polka dot dress and straw hat standing in the umpire's launch behind us shaking her fist and yelling: "Cut your bleeding wash!" Then number 5 caught a crab and was lifted bodily out of the boat . . .

John listening to the Dutch Swing College Band at his home in Flackwell Heath (LvS)

John and I took to meeting up after school, at each other's homes. Sketching in our black notebooks, we frequented a half-timbered pub in Cookham, across the bridge from The Riversdale. We wore matching black polo necked sweaters, and, both blonde, we must have looked very particular, but I at least was not conscious of this! One night, following one of our evenings in John's bedroom at Flackwell Heath, I had a slight car accident. Driving my father's large two-tone Vandenplas home after chatting and listening to The Dutch Swing College Band with John, I was in such a state of happiness that I floated gently into the rear of a mini at a yield intersection... These were times of great unspoken intimacy.

There was a boarding house at Borlase, but as dayboys – as most pupils were – both of us cycled to school. During our random chatting in our final school year, we formed the idea of cycling to Rome. Both of us were in thrall to a charismatic art teacher, and I think – as is corroborated by my journal recording the trip – our plan was to visit a chain of great works of art and architecture. At that stage John and I were set on becoming architects, but at a late moment I switched to Fine Art, which – as it turned out – merely delayed my architectural education for a year.

John and I drifted apart after going to different universities, starting families, and establishing rather different careers. We reconnected as I retired after being in practice for 15 years and being in academia for 35. John had retired a decade earlier in 2009 from 40 years as an architect concentrating on buildings associated with the physical, mental, educational, and social wellbeing of people in UK and around the world. The idea of making a record of our cycle trip arose. Leon had a handwritten journal, some photos and drawings, John had many more photos and drawings; and we both had fond memories.

Why did this project appeal? I think the answer is captured in an email exchange once we had begun. I wrote to John on 15 December 2020:

"One of my mother's gurus wrote that love never goes away. Where could it go? Transcribing days 1 and 2, 6 and 7 May as I now know, I realise how much we built together. And how it did not go away... Just underlay my later life."

John replied:

"Ref your email starting with your mum's gurus, we did indeed build a great friendship. As already inferred in stuff I've sent in connection with Trip64, for me it was that when you turned up at Borlase you were so different from other friends I had at the time – broader thinking, interested in things that spanned both the arts and sciences, completely different early

years to what I was used to, etc. What I gained from all this has underpinned what I have done subsequently. Having recently re-met you nothing has changed and it's great attempting to write the book together."

I continued:

"I am plodding on, but at the weekend I had a facetime chat with our dear friends in Western Australia, Geoffrey and Joan London. He recently retired and is an Emeritus Prof of Architecture at UWA. Joan is an award-winning novelist. I told them about our venture and about my approach to transcribing. I explained how long stretches of bicycling focus are interspersed with anecdotes such as one that ends with an elderly German exclaiming "So that's why they won the war!" They both immediately said that this must be our book title! Grab potential readers' attention! And I got echoes of your father's exploits in the background. My uncles too, one of whom was a rear gunner in a Lancaster bomber and survived. Another fought against Rommel in North Africa. My father who was unfit for service (born during the Spanish Flu he suffered from a septic ear infection all his life) did Officer Training. Another was too young to fight. Maybe that feeling of it being soon after the war can be given context by my adding this to my introduction.

You already do this, maybe there is more?"

There is indeed more, and it gives texture to the unease that I felt during our cycle through Germany. In 1963 on the return leg of a school exchange I visited Wolfsburg, the Volkswagen city, where I was beguiled by Alvar Aalto's lovely city library. My hosts were exchange student Dirk M and his family. One day his uncle took us to lunch in a luxurious restaurant on the edge of a lake in Hamburg, and on the way there, he drove us along the River Elbe on which some grand villas had survived the wartime bombing. Although I did not know it then, at about the same time the author W. G. Sebald was visiting Freiburg further up the Elbe to the northwest. Born five months earlier than me, he was preparing to study German and English literature at the university there. This, according to biographer Carole Angier, is what he found:

Some time that summer he (Sebald) went to Freiburg to find a room. This was no easy task. The city had been so badly bombed during the war that housing was still scarce; several hundred young people had to give up their university places because they couldn't find anywhere to live ...

In 1965, Dirk M inadvertently, as will emerge, confirmed in me my strongest desires.

And, so we continued, not without hiccups. But we reached agreement. What appeals to me about the project

now? I find the descriptions of each day's journey builds towards a climax in each of the sections. There is a lyricism in the account of early summer in rural Germany, and each of the Italian cities has its own hue. The need to describe qualities of space and material has become ever more pressing as digital technologies have supplanted traditional ways of crafting design instructions about what is to be made or built or printed. There may be something in these 'thick descriptions' that could assist us in making better descriptions.

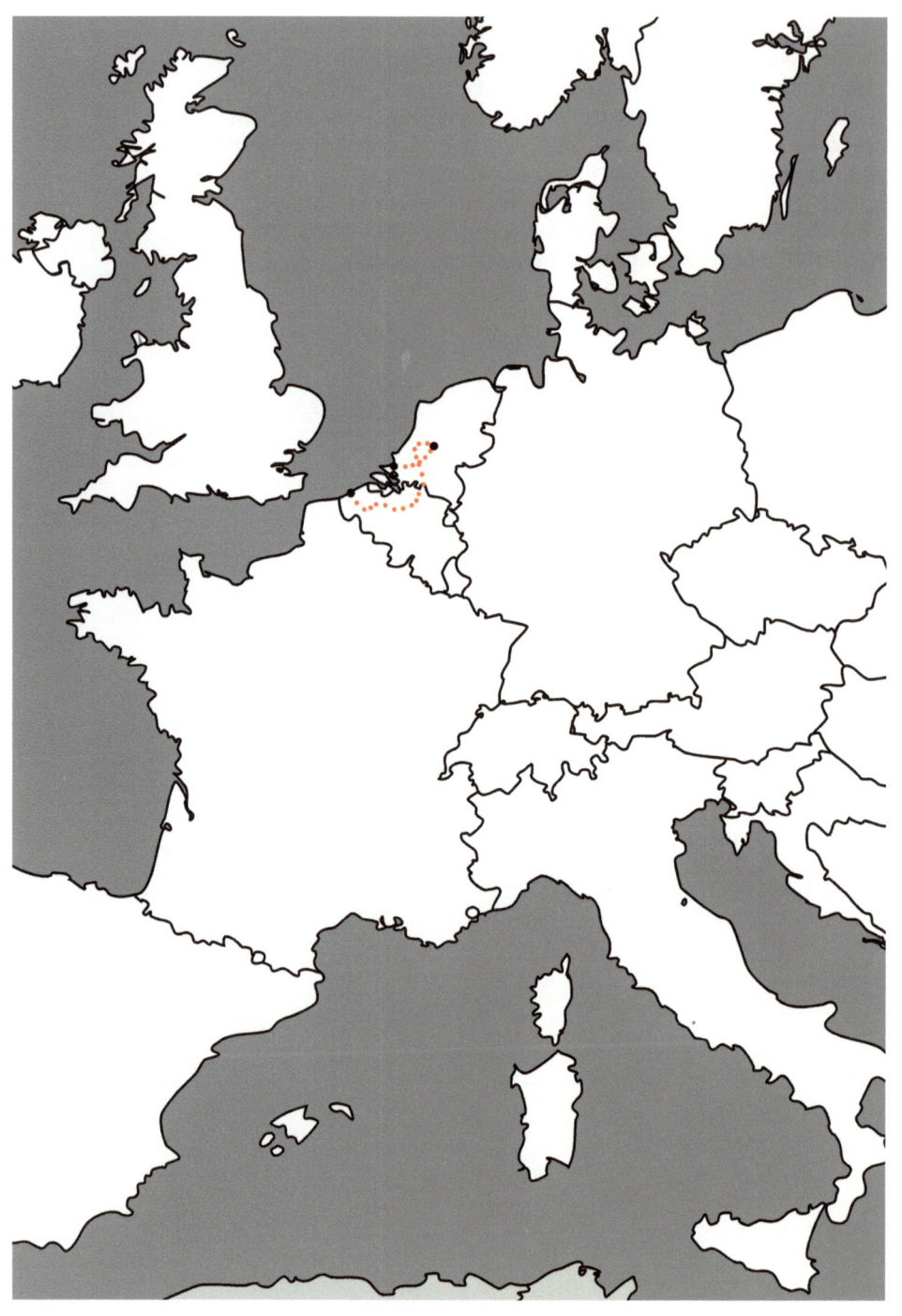

Leon: Ostend to Amsterdam and John: Hook of Holland to Amsterdam

TIMELINE PART 1 - BELGIUM / NETHERLANDS

Note re Youth Hostels: First one was established in Germany in 1909, the first in England was in 1931. The Youth Hostel movement was linked to the Peace Society, and Stanley Baldwin launched the YHA in 1936 mentioning that fact. We had to join the YHA and carry a carnet.

| Day 1<br>06 May | Bourne End to Oostende | Trains: Bourne End-Maidenhead-Paddington-London St Pancras-Dover (1h55m 108km) Bicycles allowed on GWR trains with a reservation purchased with ticket. Panniers must be removed. Bicycles allowed on underground between 9.30 and 16.00<br>Ferry: Dover-Ostend (2h51m)<br>YH Ostend on the coast Jeugdherberg De Ploate, Langestraat 72 |
|---|---|---|
| Day 2 | Oostende to Brugge Ascension Day parade | E on N377A, avoiding A10. 1h11.<br>Europa Jeugdherberg Baron Ruzettelaan 143 |
| Day 3 | Brugge to Gent | E on N337, avoiding E10, to Knesselare, then on N461 to Zomergem, then SE on Kruisstraatt via Kruisstraat to Lovendgem. Then E along Koning Leopoldstraat on north bank of canal to Brugge. 2h50.<br>Monasterium Poort Ackere hostel (now a restaurant) |
| Day 4 | Gent to Antwerp | Avoiding A14, E along the River Scheldt on N9 to Dendermonde via café near Sint Amands and Wetteren. Willebroek, A12 to Boom, then take N148, Niel, Hemiksen, Hoboken, Middelheim Park. 3h38m<br>YH Antwerp |
| Day 5 | Antwerp | YH Antwerp |
| Day 6 | Antwerp to border with Holland to Bergen op Zoom | YH Bergen op Zoom, afternoon loop to Steenbergen avoiding A4. YH Bergen op Zoom. 1h56m. |

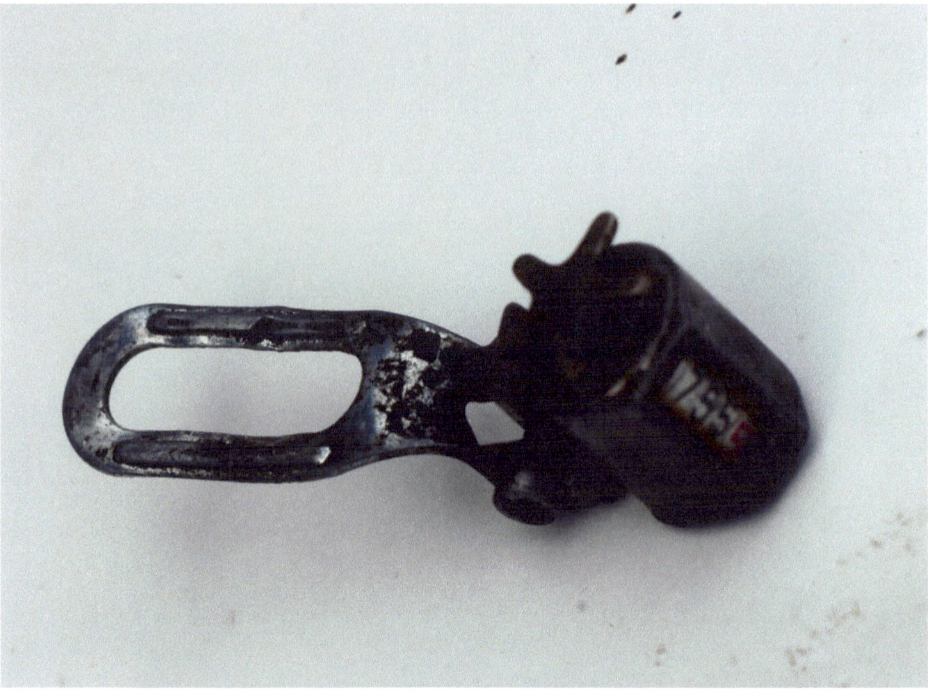

(above) John's mileometer
(below) John's paniers

| | | |
|---|---|---|
| Day 7 | To Zierikzee (where Oupa van Schaik grew up) | YH Bergen op Zoom, St Philipsland, N257 through reclamation, ferry to Brunisse, then Nieuwerkerk and Zierekzee. Back via Nieuw Vossemeer, earth track to Halsteren, bridge to Tholen, return to Halsteren and YH in de Heide. 3h13. |
| Day 8 | Middelburg / Vlissingen / Domburg | South out of Bergen op Zoom ghosting the A58 westwards to Kloetinge and Goes. Then to Middelburg and Vlissingen. Then 16 km to YH at Domberg on the North Sea coast. 3h58. |
| Day 9 | Veere / Goes / Bergen op Zoom / Wouw / Roosendaal / Breda | North out of Domberg and then east across farmlands to Veere. South to Middelburg. East to Goes and Bergen op Zoom. Loop NE to Wouw and on to Roosendaal and Breda. SE to Chaam. Return via Ginneken. Head NE to Terheijden. Sleep out near Terheijden. 6h58. |
| Day 10 | Dordrecht | Terheijden north on the A16, crossing Hollands Diep. YH Dordrecht. City centre, three rivers junction. 1h28. |
| Day 11 | Rotterdam | Dordecht north on A16 to Rotterdam. The Lijnbaan. YH Rotterdam 1h31. |
| Day 12 | Rotterdam | YH Rotterdam |
| Day 13 | To Gouda | YH Rotterdam, via Van Nelle Factory northeast to Gouda. YH Gouda. 1h29. |
| Day 14 | Den Haag (The Hague) | YH Gouda west ghosting the A12 to Den Haag. Country House YH Rijswijk, city centre. 1h51. |
| Day 15 | Scheveningen / Den Haag | Country House YH Rijswijk, city centre museums, up the coast to seaside Scheveningen, Maritiushuis, Country House YH Rijswijk 36m. |
| Day 16 | Delft | Country House YH southeast to Delft. Return to Country House YH Rijswijk. 1h10. |
| Day 17 | Leiden | Country House YH Rijswijk northeast to Leiden YH Kaag 1h48. |

TIMELINE PART 1

| | | |
|---|---|---|
| Day 18 | Keukenhof (tulips over) / Haarlem / Bloemendaal / Zandvoort / Ijmuiden | YH Kaag north to Keukenhof, north to Haarlem, Jan Gijzen Hostel south to Bloemendal, Zandvoort, Jan Gijzen Hostel. 1h54. |
| Day 19 | To Amsterdam, | Jan Gijzen Hostel east on A200 to Amsterdam, 101 Jan van Galenstraat. 1h50. |
| Day 20 | Amsterdam - 1 | 101 Jan van Galenstraat |
| Day 21 | Amsterdam - 2 | 101 Jan van Galenstraat (Tane Greta) |
| Day 22 | Amsterdam - 3 | 101 Jan van Galenstraat |
| Day 23 | Marken (Costume village) / Monnickendam / Volendam / Kwadijk / Alkmaar / Schoorl, | 101 Jan van Galenstraat, ferry to Utdammerdijk along the Ijmeer to island of Marken, then Monnickendam, Volendam, east inland to Kwadijk cont. east to Alkmaar, then northeast to YH Schoorl, which is full, so east to YH Oosterdijk on the Ijsselmeer. 3h30 |
| Day 24 | Oosterdijk / Afsluitdijk / Alkmaar / Zaandam / Amsterdam | YH Oosterdijk northwest to Afsluitdijk 2h44. (A7). Southwest to Alkmaar, 3h17, south past Zaandam to Amsterdam, YH Amsterdam. 2h17. Total=8h18 |
| Day 25 | Amsterdam - 4 | 101 Jan van Galenstraat |
| Day 26 31 May | Amsterdam - 5 Meet John! | 101 Jan van Galenstraat |

TIMELINE PART 1

DAY 1
WEDNESDAY MAY 06
BOURNE END / LONDON VICTORIA / DOVER / OSTEND

Was not seasick.

Leon: Prided myself on my sea legs ever since my first crossing on a school skiing trip in December 1962. We left England the day The Big Freeze covered the country in snow, and arrived in Steinach – to a snowless Austria ...

Ostend.
Opulent apartment blocks along the coast.

John: During a drive back from a trip to Brugge a few years ago we drove past these blocks and, like much of the Belgian coast on the Straits of Dover, the area was very industrialized and had lost the post-war enthusiasm to replace destruction by a brighter and better environment like the one Leon would have seen in 1964.

I wander out, lost. Where is the Youth Hostel? I cycle a bit, turning when I feel I've gone too far. Pass French looking parks; white-painted and shuttered shops. I stop to ask two taxi men the way – in my Afrikaans. They tell me, in English ... "It's out along the coast, behind the apartment strip." Big cars ripple past, their tyres thumping over the little blocks used for road surfacing. Lots of American cars. Peugeots seem to wear well, and so do Citroens.

Leon: Rusting chrome and door sills were commonplace in cars then. As I was tasked with cleaning the family cars, I knew all too well the tell-tale signs: bubbling chrome, the crumbling seams below doors ...

To my eyes, the Youth Hostel is old and slummy.
Having a meal at the communal table I meet a German and an American. They tell me that they have been working in a Lutheran mission at Rugby.
Also meet Katerin.
She's beautiful.

Leon: Via Borlase in 1963 I met Dirk from Wolfsburg, who was visiting a family nearby to improve his English. Without understanding this, I was smitten.

We all sing along with guitar, German drinking songs and one in English about living off the earnings of a high-class lady.
In the dorm I meet a Swede who studies Sanskrit.
Much talk.

Leon: The first Swede I'd met

DAY 2
THURSDAY MAY 07
BRUGGE (BRUGES)

Cycle in pouring rain. Rear wheel carrier kept breaking down.

Leon: I had strapped a waterproof sleeping bag and a change of clothes and toiletries to single carriers over the rear and front wheels...and a tent?

John: I had our only tent on my bike dammit! At some point we posted it home because we hardly ever used it and it was heavy on my bike

Country green and flat and boring ... oh, I was prejudiced by the drizzle. Keep seeing this sign on fences: 'Nog een Cools skrikdraad' (yet another electric fence by Cools, literally 'shock wire'), and (head down) and without knowing it, I reach Brugge.

    I round a corner of the street and encounter a gatehouse on the circling canal. The canal banks are grassed and lined with trees in spring leaf.

    Houses down both sides, white and grey small-chateau style, older gothic gabled ones and later Victorian ones interspersed.

    I stopped and looked and looked. Still raining. A lady smiled at me, I smiled back, wet through.

    A burgundy colour two-door Citroen DS floats by

Leon: One of a string of dream cars that I never owned. I recall boasting to John that my dad was getting one of the new P5 Rovers and John mocking me when what arrived was a two-tone VandenPlas – and later a two-tone Rover Coupe. Eventually I got a red Citroen Dyane and later a chrome yellow Lancia. Cars obsessed me from early childhood, when they were all American, and later, when more eco-minded, I had Prius Hybrids, and now hope for an all-electric or hydrogen vehicle.

John: My Introduction declares my love of the Spitfire fighter plane but, until collaborating on this book, I did not know about Leon's love for the Citroen DS. My love for this car is the same as that for the Spitfire. My next car love was a 1951 MG TD and I now have my third love, a 1987 Renault 4 which I bought in 2002 and still use every day.

I walked on and on and wandered all day till in the afternoon the sun came out and dried me.

    All the tricks are used in Brugge.

Leon: I was thinking of the twists and turns of the brick footpaths in old parts of Marlow towards the weir.

John: One of these behind the church was called "snog-alley" because it had two right angled corners between which you could "cuddle" your partner. Another brick

footpath from near Borlase down towards the rowing club was called "dogshit-alley" for obvious reasons.

A row of houses – enchanting – and you see greenery beyond them and walk on, towards a square, which it sometimes is or it's not a square, just a tree over a wall; and the abiding centre of interest is the canal, then seen again.

Encounter the Holy Blood Procession: terribly solemn, the whole town seems to be there.

Christ in all his stages depicted by men rolling their eyes to heaven, red chins to the earth. Sometimes I wanted to laugh, but no one else did. Each float had its own canned music, now Alibaba, now heavenly choir. Marvellously groomed horses, their black coats combed into chequers. The relic, a forearm (!) came by, followed by the bishop on his own float, kneeling. Suddenly I was the only one standing.

> Leon: Wikipedia – "In 2009 this 'Heilig Bloedprocess', a large religious Catholic procession dating back to the Middle Ages, which takes place each Ascension Day in Bruges, Belgium, was included in the UNESCO Representative List of the Intangible Cultural History of Humanity." Only a few tens of miles from home, but utterly otherworldly. I recall an Afrikaner nationalist who headed for Holland hoping to find his spiritual home, and discovering that all was strange, while in England all was familiar.

Bought a bun and ham – 5 francs plus 1 franc for being English.

Walked all over town until my feet ached; watched barges drift through the drawbridges of the canal. Some canalside houses have entrances of dark double doors leading through tunnels to glimpses of gardens. As I walk past small houses, curtains twitch, once a woman leans out.

Inside houses are crammed with brass, with pots and potted plants, carpets – 'oosterse tapijten', lace. Brown paint predominates. There are old people and young children. 'Wonderlik'.

Find the Europa Jeugdherberg. The warden is very Flemish. "Van Schaik? But that is a Dutch name..." Meet disillusioned Australians here. Enjoined by one into going for a beer, rich and dark brown. 17 francs for a half pint! Best we have, bustled the barwoman. Joined by a USA student who had just been refused entry to 'Blighty'. Perfidious Albion. We sat under wet canvas near the Begijnhof, looking over grass, through willows, at earthy swans... A party of Dutch girls came. Bells rang. More bells...

I undertook an agonised reappraisal of the packing of my kit.

DAY 3
FRIDAY MAY 08
GHENT

Cycle through rows of trees accompanied by an English cyclist who is heading to Israel. The repacked bicycle behaves...

We pass farmhouses with painted shutters, encounter a long hill and after Zomergem we reach Lovendgem, passing priests walking along an avenue towards a canal. Flicked by sunshine through leaves we followed the canal, passing barges. Above lily ponds loomed a shuttered baroque minor gentry chateau.

Cycling down a long canal we reached the centre of Ghent at 11.30, coming to two big churches at the centre, against one of which there were porcelain urinals with men casually and openly pissing...

Leon: I became very familiar with this area visiting it twice yearly in the early 21st century, a model of inner-urban renewal.

Took leave of my (nameless) cycling friend and – pushing my bike – walked the town till 4.30. Looser urban fabric than Brugge with suburbs of bungalows that reminded me of childhood Johannesburg. At the centre I note the terrace houses, a castle, chestnut trees, shady squares paved from side to side with no demarcations – unlike the rule-defined surfaces in London. Reflect that without these divisions of surface building talks to building.

Ghent leads you on, but sometimes – unlike Brugge – lets down its guard. Looks familiar at moments, an overgrown Maidenhead.

Leon: Given the history of Ghent, the second largest city in Europe in the 13th century, rich on processing wool from East Anglia, this was a rawly naive comparison with a town near home. And "two big churches"! One of these houses Jan van Eyck's Adoration of the Lamb 1429. Not noted.

Ask police the way to the Youth Hostel, which is in an old monastery.

Leon: Here in this same building in the early 21st century the members of my RMIT PhD program, hosted by St Lucas School of Architecture, ate some very strange, entirely grey meals.

Meet four very spirited Australian girls who claimed to have been everywhere.

Have a cold shower, glow with a marvellous feeling of physical well-being. Huge supper of soup, steak and chips, pineapple. (Have cut out lunch as too expensive. Can do

without.) More Americans. One claimed that South Africans talked only about home. The others had been 'over' since October, working in a kibbutz. Wandering after supper I saw the English flagged barge – a 'botter' with retractable side rudders – that I first saw in Brugge. Dad would love it!

```
DAY 4
SATURDAY MAY 09
ANTWERP VIA DENDERMONDE
```

At 8.30 I jolt out of Ghent on cobbled roads. As I approach Wetteren I find myself in a lovely country – in a flat way. Ranks of trees flit past as I approach the river Schelde. In the dusty brick town, there is a procession of schoolchildren led by priests and two solemn youths bearing flags. Ribbon development (the unplanned process that enabled mass housing construction in the interwar years) hides the river. The houses are modernist. Then near St Amands I enter pleasant, wooded country.

Take a break at Cafe t'Paradijs. The name says everything about it! The break, that is.

Two kilometres before Willebroek I join a dual carriageway. Smooth passage halted by a lift bridge over a canal. Waiting, I chat to a Belgian boy who tells me that he has been to Romford in Essex: "the cigarettes were so expensive!"

"Ha! Cigarettes," think I, as every day here I long for a beer, but it is too expensive. Every day I long for an orange. Also, out of reach of my daily budget ...

I take what on my map looks to be a pleasant secondary road into Antwerp, via Boom. Enter the city via Niel, dykes lined with houses rising above waves of long tiled sheds; the tiles of all colours, green and new orange intermingled. Rejects, I guess. Little trains run between the sheds, clouds of smoke blow across, laughter floats up. This goes on for miles! It is the brickworks.

Back in the countryside I see how the canal banks are kept from eroding by staking willow weave hurdles one above another. Horses still very much in evidence, working farms, pulling delivery carts. One such is hitched to two Alsatian dogs. Old men hobble in clogs. They are wearing berets and wide corduroy trousers. These are not isolated instances, there are many! Elsewhere though, clogs are for decoration and tourists. And shops have a wider range of consumer goods than ours, more sense of design. Men's clothing strikes me as stylish, even the garish stuff is tastefully so. Pissoirs are simply stuck to walls. No screening only the side view is blocked ...

Reach Hemiksen and Hoboken. Houses, three stories high and with blank gable walls, hope for neighbours. When will they join the ribbon? Reach Middeheim, a park on the outskirts of Antwerp. It struck me as lovely, but I was sore all over from cycling and made for the Youth Hostel. It has a moat on three sides and faces new housing on the far bank. An

office building suspended from its core drew my attention. I find the screens particularly interesting and take a photograph – my first (!) As I find to be common practice here, poplar saplings are planted two feet apart and their tops are lopped off, sometimes at third storey height.

Wolf down an enormous meal sitting next to a talkative American girl and a taciturn Dutchman. Meet Australians Ron and a girl with a sprained ankle and help them to the washroom where we nurse our feet. Later an English yob seeing that I was reading my map bawled out: "What's that? A Map!!!Good Lord No!!" Two American couples fresh from Holland joined us. Much talk.

I haven't drawn much. And I don't want to feel obliged to. Subjects for me are few. I have the horrid feeling that I am doing this trip for nothing – but suppress it. Decide to spend the next day resting.

DAY 5
SUNDAY MAY 10
ANTWERP

I walk out fresh and early – a lovely day – ready to be led where the city wills it. I pass well-upholstered terrace houses; wander through streets looking at windows and at my reflection in windows; come to the centre. The Museums don't interest me today, and anyway they are closed. Come to a big square surrounded by beer houses which spill over in neat platforms onto the pavement. Lots of old people on benches.
    Leon:    I wonder what 'old' meant to this 19-year-old?
Down narrow streets I am released into a tight triangular space over which towers the cathedral. Through an escape hatch I reach another quieter square, again with pavement beer houses on one side, Italianate gothic town hall on another side and Dutch houses step-gabled around. In the centre is a fountain. It has no basin. Rises in three storeys of squirming statuary. Water gushes from where a man's head has been torn off AND from where his head is. Grotesque but delicious, water falling directly onto the cobbles then runs back under the statue. Wander up a seedy back alley and a view of old stone draws me down a little tunnel seeking an old building only to find the River Schelde popped up under a bridge across the road, and so that's where I am going.
    It's getting hot. Walk along a promenade above the docks. Watch HMS City of Liverpool dock. Shall I shout: "Yoo-hoo, I'm English?" No, I shall not. I hear brass bands everywhere – yes. It's another capital P procession. Walk to the noise and see local dignitaries being led to their station by a smartly turned-out band. Solemn crowd watches, the street is head lined. The band strikes up with 'Knees up mother brown'! No one finds it amusing. I could burst – fancy the cardinal doing the hokey cokey! This time placards reveal that the serious faced kids in the procession are campaigning for 'Welvaart'. The event lasts for hours – it feels – and adds up to a definite statement that 'it's not fair.' I hope that "they" are watching.
    I love chestnut trees. I keep walking towards them down streets – only they are usually behind walls. Think that Antwerp must be a good city to live in. Most blocks crust a private park, more trees behind walls. Lawns I see through tunnel entrances. Walk through a district of three to four storey terraces interspersed with churches and squares covered by three to four chestnut trees. Kids play hopscotch. Old men doze. It is sweltering. Every street has a cool and inviting corner bar. Who or what is Stella Artois? Billiard balls

knock lazily. I dream of cool vats of beer and settle for 4-franc Granny Smith which I eat for lunch in a park.

I wish I had a Union Jack, then everyone would understand that although I look like a native, I am not from here. Here they are in their Sunday best, they've been to church, they've watched the procession and I'm in jeans and sandals, tut, tut! In the afternoon I am still walking. It's quieter, everyone seems to drift to the sea front and so do I. A sailor is propped against a wall, drunk. I could die for a beer. My feet are now raw. Head back to the hostel through quiet streets. People are washing cars. "Can I drink your water?" Reach the Youth Hostel.

Supper at a local restaurant, delicious and plenty. Pork, beans, potatoes and soup. Can they cook here! 30 francs, but at last I am spending and what's 7 francs more? I have a pils. A Yank joins me. Over-cultured, but he likes Tapies . . .

Holland tomorrow!

<u>DAY 6</u>
<u>MONDAY MAY 11</u>
<u>LEAVING ANTWERP / BERGEN-OP-ZOOM</u>

I left early, leaving Antwerp at 8.30, cycling along ribbon development which never let up. I did catch glimpses of rustic scenery between the villas but was bored. The road was dead straight. Suddenly there was the sign DOUANE. I wavered about a bit and then a man in uniform waved me on – I was in the NETHERLANDS! Same street, same houses! Oh no! But no, it quickly changed, the ribboning ended, and I was in some of the most beautiful, wooded countryside that I have seen. Tante Greta and Oom Karel would later tell me that this was the hill country of the Netherlands. High up on a hill I saw what the Dutch in the Cape were aiming at and what had so often failed when they moved north: gabled, verandah-ed and shuttered houses with tree screens in front. These set pieces popped up all the way to Bergen-op-Zoom. The Netherlands being thrillingly Nederland. Special.

Bergen-op Zoom is a hilly country town with its gatehouse and marketplace and streets of small houses all set about with chestnut trees. There is a Boer Bank and a Boer Winkel (Farmer Bank and Farmer Shop). At a bank I changed my money (from Belgian francs), understanding the teller and he me when we spoke 'stadig' (slowly). It all feels more friendly than Flanders; unsolicited a postman greets me and – a first this – girls wolf-whistle at me. I am amazed! At home girls only seem to go for the dark haired and tuberculoid! I see me in many faces. My gene-pool...

The Youth Hostel in the middle of a large wood I find quite un-institutional – a welcome change. I leave my baggage and wander through the nearby countryside, finding wide horizons, trees in clusters, trees in rows, barns at right-angles to their shuttered farmhouses with tulip filled gardens, lead clad church towers within clustered villages, men and women in blue overalls working fields. I am so carried away with looking that I nearly cycle into a ditch.

In villages all through traffic is kept away, there are children in the streets. I see more children in an afternoon than in three years in England.

At Steenberg an enormous church with a conical steeple looms up on my horizon. Here there is a lot of new housing in clusters and parkland runs all the way through. It seems very liveable. From one end the main street seems to dead-end onto a neoclassical – hence 18th century – church. At the last moment the road swings. From the other side the road seems to head straight up into an ordinary shopping street, only it

doesn't, it feints left into a civic parade, and then – through a gap halfway along – there is the church set in chestnuts. It gives me pleasure to glide through. I recognise the term 'Slagerij' (Butchery).

Ride back to Bergen-op-Zoom through more wooded country. The town is now buzzing with people. Compared to England the towns are unaffected by car traffic. Why? There is rigid streaming of traffic. 'Lokale verkeer' and 'Doorgaand verkeer' are separated. Bicycle paths are distinct and well signed. Every village has worked out its solution. It all works so well that it makes the mess back home seem pathetic. West Brabant seems so civil and egalitarian. Love it.

At the hostel, now crowded with Dutch travellers, I talk to a padre in my limited Afrikaans and am not taken to task for the backwoods simplicity of the dialect . . .

Zierikzee: The gatehouse to the old city, the harbour beyond (LvS)

```
DAY 7
TUESDAY MAY 12
TO ZIERIKZEE
```

Cycle out from Bergen-op-Zoom against the wind, trudge-pedalling through miles of flat, lusciously green and treed agricultural land, dotted with horses and cows. Villages are well spread out; each layout includes a church and a windmill.

```
    Leon:       This was my first encounter with the regularity of
                spatial arrangements that gave rise to Central Place
                Theory with its evenly graduated nesting of hamlet/
                village/ town/city.
```

At St. Phillipsland, I reach polder country. The road is sometimes on a dyke, sometimes in a ditch. Farmsteads have green and white shutters and big brick and thatch barns, gardens with tulips and chestnut shaded courtyards.

I cross on the ferry. Think much of Oupa, my grandfather: Zierikzee, so remote, especially in an age without cars, better be good to have kept its young. Well, it didn't, did it? But first Niewekerk, another fine village in which old and new fit well together. The countryside has become slightly monotonous. At last! Zierikzee greets me with undistinguished brick terrace house lined streets. I go on, sinking heart, and come to a gatehouse that blocks the view. Cycle through, and it's a gem! The old harbour is surrounded by 18th century houses; there is a marketplace and a church where my great, great grandfather was Kapellmeister. There is a new harbour outside the old town, also surrounded by houses. Drawbridges link quaysides lined with sea-going boats. There are two more gatehouses, alleys. Brimming with pride: 'My Oupa was hier gebore" I tell the lady in the postcard shop. "Nou ja" she says quietly. A dismissive 'Oh yes?'. The medieval core does not disappoint. Mum and Dad – you must visit!

```
    Leon:       Years later my aunt Betty gave me a family tree
                and a map of Zierekzee showing the houses that the
                family had lived in. On the day, I was imagining my
                grandfather playing in the main street and wondering
                which house he grew up in. Have felt no desire to
                return to look at the actual house.
```

Back on winding agricultural roads through Nieuw Vossemeer. Clumps and rows of trees, black and white Friesland cows in deep green fields, people relaxing on verandas. Hilly after a bit, chestnut surrounded thatched barns, a wagon pulled by great placid farm horses. I approach Halsteren on a dirt track, a village with the usual ingredients but also with new housing set in parkland. Bicycle showing worrying signs of wear, but I can see the bridge leading to Tholen on the horizon, and I

deviate to this lovely village in hills with old houses set about a tree'd green and an English looking church with a Dutch tower. People everywhere.

Back through the twilight to my favourite hostel parents, a young couple who run the hostel without rules. I have supper alone in the kitchen beside the gas stove. The hall is occupied by a club, this night. Sit and talk with 'moeder en vader' until 11.30, me snatching sense from the Dutch here and there. In the hall, 'vader' leads boys and girls in singing South African songs which embarrass rather than reassure me: My Sarie Marais, Die Khakies (?), Hold him down you Zulu warrior! Shepherding the children is a round plat Dutch assistant. Moeder has two screaming sons. Tells me what to see – if not yet seen.

```
DAY 8
WEDNESDAY MAY 13
TO VLISSINGEN AND DOMBURG VIA MIDDELBURG
```

Set out early, it turned into a good day, but the wind is against me.

Continue to enjoy the hill country from Bergen-op-Zoom to Goes, the church of which I saw through miles of apple and cherry tree orchards, all in blossom and screened by windbreaks of poplar trees. The occasional wild apple tree on the road verge. Sunshine, green fields, what more?

Kloetinge and Goes are attractive towns with ponds, tree'd parks, old houses and windmills. A sprinkling of new houses. Then I leave the hills and the country is flat and I struggle against the wind. At last I reach Middelburg, attractive too, but I head for Vlissingen and the hostel. Ribbon development all the six kilometres and I arrive depressed and find a port and new town. The Youth Hostel is right under a windmill, but it's closed. Face a sixteen-kilometre ride to Domburg. The sea here is up there over the dyke. It's odd watching people walk up to the beach. I think of Durban, the most dramatic approach to the sea that I know: town, town, town up a broad tarmac street and there it lies! Stretching forever...

I miss a signpost and approach Biggarkereks over an unmade road. Must get to Domburg for the evening meal! More pleasant villages and then Domburg! A sunny evening and there are visiting farm people in their Sunday best in the town square. I do get a meal in the hostel shack, sitting beside a 'buxom wench' who has cycled from Amsterdam. She used just the right English words: "Josh! Jolly! Jracious!" Also, four Rotterdam youths of 14 years, one of whom spoke English really well. I walked to the beach over a natural sand barrier that – seen from miles inland – had looked like a mountain range. Ships on the horizons. Back to bed, drop off quickly, dead tired and sore. The boys come in late. "De Engelsman slaap." Talk of 'sexuale honger." Nou ja. I sleep late.

Cycling into the wind on dead flat roads (LvS)

```
DAY 9
THURSDAY MAY 14
TO VEERE / BREDA
```

In the morning to Veere. Boring country. Sail (following wind!) into a village and find facing a windmill a row of fine old houses next to a quay, and in the square a magnificent one with gothic stepping gables and carvings. Otherwise, disappointing, and the road to Middelburg is frightful! Dead straight! Unchanging trees! For seven kilometres! I'm asleep on the pedals. Was this all worth it? Middelburg cloyed. Too much quaint decay. Little variety. Still, I find fine houses around the harbour and a circular plan church. Back with the wind behind me and my spirits rise as I reach Goes. The scent of blossom is overpowering. In Bergen-op-Zoom I buy a new saddle.

    It turns into a great day on which everything went wrong, but no matter... calm, hot weather, French girls at the Hostel spent time photographing me – or pretending to! I was the only male. Rode exhilarated to Wouw along an avenue of trees, dappled sunshine. Wouw high street makes a right-angle turn (around the church). Ride to Rosendaal, which is new and bare. So new, that street signs are still being erected. No new architectural or planning ideas in the new shopping centre.

    Into Breda, which I love. Giant chestnut trees shading parks are in flower, new housing alongside slums, no individual building outstanding. A fantastic amount of building going on in the old quarter – addressing subsidence? Out to Chaam in the heat of the afternoon through a very attractive wooded country. Soldiers eye me enviously. Men and women are hoeing the fields. The Hostel is full, so back to Breda. Two punctures, stop, fix, have beer – a Pils served from an earthenware jug. Cycle through quiet residential Ginneken. See this sign: "C. van Schaik, Tandarts" (Dentist). Yes, but as if all the Smiths in the world knew each other!

    Supper at Chris's Chip Stall and cycle out to Terheidjen. At a roundabout a Volkswagen Combi van keels over so far that it hits a lamp pole broadside on. Heineken Beer everywhere. People sit on their verandas watching the evening go by. Chestnuts are heavy with foliage, white walls, euphorically I could extend the moment forever. Maybe it's the beer? Men in corduroy walking. Kids are swimming in a pond. Nearly knocked into by a huge farm horse. So is an old lady. Ride high up onto a bridge over a canal, sunsetting, a barge put-putting a wake. Stand and watch, feeling at peace. Look for a camping spot along a luscious dyke, planted lusciously with trees.

Stepped gable, brick and thatch and green shuttered farmhouses sit on individual islands, each reached by a drawbridge. At one, a man leans on the bridge gate smoking a pipe, I push my bike up to him and try to say how beautiful – "mooi' – the scene is. "You are not sleeping with my daughter!" he shouts at me. I end up in my waterproof bag alongside a swamp.

DAY 10
FRIDAY MAY 15
DORDRECHT

Sleep fitfully till 5.00 AM and make on through the rain to Dordrecht, which I reach in rush-hour and all the world is a Volkswagen van. Monotonous ride, dead straight road. Can hardly summon up the interest to pedal. But the bridge over the 'Hollandse Diep', affords a wide, over the water view of boats.

Dordrecht. Regimented housing estates, flats screened with trees. To the hostel for a wash, through shrub-suburb. Shruburbia. Town very depressing. All in the same brick, and I don't like decay for decay's sake, filthy roads, broken windows ... But there is a magnificent windmill and at the dock area great patriarch houses surround two long harbour canals full of small ships. Backyard workshops serving the docks are busy. Reach the shopping area, but I am tired and bored and sit in a park under a tree watching lunch hour kids and antelopes. Homesick. Walk the bicycle past little houses, looking in. People look out. They're chock-a-block with stuff. Stifling. Kids can't play inside. Much building in progress. Flashy new building near the station. Lots of shops selling little bits for the inside of stifling houses where children can't play. They're very friendly though, the kids. It drizzles. I worry about the future and how secure. Endless pots of free tea. Can't control my legs. Find through a decaying gateway the meeting point of three rivers and watch some of the 1200 barges said to pass each day. This I love doing. A cruiser flagged for the USA is in dock. It's cold. Handwritten sign on a collapsing house: For Sale. Stumble back to the hostel and drown sorrows in a bottle of Si-Si lemonade. The Dutch are very Italy conscious.

DAY 11
SATURDAY MAY 16
TO ROTTERDAM

Dordrecht looks happy in the sunlight. (I am happy in the sunshine. I am happy to be on the move again.)
    Cycle in the company of three Dutch nurses from Bergen-op-Zoom and a South African who talked about the USA all the way. We took the bridge over the river and from that height all falls into place: a church towers over the port on an inshore river, new housing lies beyond. We find the road to Rotterdam. Fairly interesting trajectory through trees and glasshouses. At last, I see cranes towing into the sky and a ship passing high above the horizon. Close up the cranes are red tubular structures working on a matrix across a concrete apron. More new housing and then old, trees, the centre! Disappointing at first. There is no actual centre, new buildings in a grid do not hang together in the organic way that I have become accustomed to in un-bombed towns. Much construction on the go, but it's hard to tell. Down an old street arcing along a tree-lined canal and find at last the centre that I was expecting. The Lijnbaan.

Leon:     I note that John made his way to this too. It must have been on our architectural list. My father had designed a shopping street on the same principles in the 1950s. Its unroofed street pattern was superseded by the mall model promoted by Victor Gruen. Two decades later I revisited it, finding it newly restored.

John:     I did indeed visit the Lijnbaan shopping centre during my second day in Holland on 29 May as I describe under Leon's Day 24.

I like the Lijnbaan. Good design works. At "House of England" people are sitting outside drinking.
    Find the fine hostel and meet up with my Austrian 'friend' Peter Flora – son of Paul Flora (1922–2009) the cartoonist for The Times, The Observer and Die Zeit.

Leon:     While I wrote 'friend' this indicated a mutual recognition, I think. I expected to continue this friendship by correspondence, but in the rush of new experiences at university, did not. Peter Flora (b. 3 March 1944) went on to become professor of sociology at the University of Mannheim, retiring in 2009. He wrote Growth to Limits: The Western European Welfare State Since World War II (1986). This was a missed opportunity analogous to that of my never developed friendship with Roger Sandilands at Borlase. He, who I remembered as an attractive person, light-hearted and

amiable, and blonde - was by then emeritus professor of economics at the university of Strathclyde - contacted me in May 2014 having heard my name during a discussion on architecture in Edinburgh. We shared opinions on the double burning of the Glasgow School of Art. Why lost opportunities? At the height of my academic management career, I was Dean of a Faculty that was formed by a merger between Architecture and Landscape and Interior Architectures, and Construction Management, Planning, Social Science, Social Work and Socio-environmental policy. I named it the Faculty of the Constructed Environment - physically, socially and politically constructed. It was an academically fruitful period. These glancing connections could have enriched it further!

We were amongst Americans awaiting boats and planes home. We all went to a carpet covered table pub. Two very happy days follow. I visit the Kalsiger dam set in woods and the building centre sporting a Henry Moore. The centre was graffitied: 'The Beatles.' Ironic juxtaposition of Anglophilias. Admired the honeycomb inspired facade of De Bijenkorf store and the Naum Gabo that it backdrops. Sat and watched kids playing around the Zadkine sculpture.

    Leon:    This evocation of the horror of the bombing has haunted my memory ever since. I had not yet seen Picasso's Guernica.

Stroll along the river looking at ships, and – in a small harbour surrounded by neoclassical houses – see yachts. Walk to the Euromast which floats over the city like a lost hovercraft. Lie in the sun in a newly landscaped park near the Maas tunnel.

    Back to the hostel, shower and then with Peter, walk through the evening to Coolsingel and Lijnbaan, talking.

DAY 12
SUNDAY MAY 17
ROTTERDAM

Buy new carriers for the bike. Meet Peter at the museum. Fascinated by early Mondriaan: squares of yellow and red on white without black lines. Also, Klees new to me. Walk through parks, sit in shade where we are mobbed by kids with grubby arms alternatively attacking us or offering sweets and daisies. Move on and watch ships. Back to the hostel which is – say two Dutch girls – undecided about its opening time . . . share tea in the common room. Over supper drawn into an involved discussion with an American philosopher who had been in England for one week – enough he declared! A German psychologist living in London countered this and opened a conversation about photo-art. Helped the Dutch girls with the washing up. "You understand Dutch? Oooh! What have you heard us saying? Aha. Not so well." Walked to Delfshaven, the oldest dock in Rotterdam. At its market watch fish buying and the skinning of live eels.

DAY 13
MONDAY MAY 18
TO GOUDA

In the morning I cycled to the Van Nelle Factory (Brinkman and van der Vlugt, 1925–1931, on our list.) Looks five years old! I find it hard to believe that it is 34 years old.

On to Gouda, through the very flat country in a heat haze. It's Sunday...

```
Leon:     Can't work out why I wrote this as clearly it was not.
          Equally clearly in the journal, it was not the day
          before.
```

...and everyone is out, on bromponies (twin stroke motorbikes), on bikes, in cars. Others are sailing on Kralingse Plas.

Approach Gouda alongside a canal, then a harbour and windmill. Dive down off the dyke into a leafy canalside street lined with old brick houses, some gothic stepped gales, some square with arch topped windows. It feels open along the canal bank, it's hot and dry when I turn into a back street. Come to a hand over hand cable operated ferry. It's all very pleasant but not spectacular until heading down a long shopping street, there it stands! A tall, yellowstone, red and white triangles shuttered house. As I move around it, it unfolds into the (restored) long and venerable Stadhuis, 1415. Stairs lead up to a first-floor canopied entrance. The shutters make a striking pattern down the long flanks and behind is a gay French style hotel with orange awnings and a cubic seventeenth century weigh-house, twin barrel vaulted over the road. I circle noting sculptures and how the Stadhuis dominates in isolated splendour, while the nearby St. Janskerk is lost in a huddle of houses.

I move on. Houses back onto canals, each with their own bridge. Visit a large, white, 17th century patrician house with a central courtyard, sort of cottage renaissance. More canals, more houses. Cycle back to the town square through the weigh house, cross the flat cobbled surface, then splendour floods in as I, looking back through the weigh house, find a view of the plain gable end of the Stadhuis, edged by a side-on yellow building. Holland doesn't often do spectacular! On through new housing, standard good, through the Wijks recreation centre: swimming, sunbathing, boating – sails everywhere. Houses down a central dyke, each with a swivel bridge. Reach the Youth Hostel, eat out with chips! Puncture. Try to fix it. Fail. Make up my bed in the hostel loft and fall asleep exhausted. Emotionally drained I dream that Dad drives up in his station wagon, puts my bike in the back, waves "goodbye old chap" and is gone. Sleep on happily. How much I rely on mum and dad!

```
DAY 14
TUESDAY MAY 19
THE HAGUE-1
```

Diarist John Evelyn (1620–1706) – who we studied at Borlase – spoke of small houses with orange trees. The vast grey blob of my map filled me with foreboding. Indeed, the town sprawls but it's filled with flowing parks and canals. Eventually, after lemonade off a barrow, I reach a centre with fine old houses screened by beech tree hedges. I can't get the map of the place into my head. Spend a happy afternoon sketching the Binnehof. Few people about. See the Peace Palace (funded by Andrew Carnegie, it opened in 1913, but looks to me as if designed in 1813, well mid-Victorian . . .) All very pleasant and floating in trees, nothing spectacular, a decent place to live I reflect. At every turn there is a street organ with its heaving plastic folk art facade. Here and in the tight streets of Dordrecht or in Rotterdam's glass faced parades; each creating its own little atmosphere, with its mechanically beating mechanical arm unfolding punched sheets.

    Even Rotterdam is shut tight after 6.00 PM. All go home to their family. Domestic routines are pervasive rituals – washing of house faces, doorsteps and the pavement, lace half-curtains neatly bunched, whitewashed onto the glass sometimes (masking poverty?), and (glimpsed) well-patterned, crammed little rooms. Religion is evident everywhere. Newspapers are paternal. Men in clogs. Service people are friendly, but there is a service charge. They are paid to be so. Will Italy be different? A jumble of impressions. Yet what do I know of Holland?

    I know how a girl in a tight skirt cycles.

    Cycle out to the Hostel. Now this is what to do with country houses!

```
Leon:    Even in wealthy home county Buckinghamshire at this
         time, many were in a state of decay with collapsing
         perimeter walls, leaking roofs...
```

With Geordies and Dutch girls, play volleyball in the fading light. Tea outside (literally tea, not the meal suggested in some English usage). Meet again the Rotterdam arguers.

DAY 15
WEDNESDAY MAY 20
THE HAGUE / SCHEVENINGEN

Straight to the GemeenteMuseum (1935, designed by H.P. Berlage) where I find 'New Babylon (1956–1976) by Constant. And the massive display of Piet Mondriaan and his influences, The Breuer chair and other Bauhaus furniture, and a replica Art Nouveau living room. Vormentaal – literally form and language – exposition of the Dutch analysis of the language of Classical Architecture – here a mix of Typography, Graphics, Blown-up photographs... Enjoy the intensely worked images of Lucebert (1924–1994), like Constant, a member of COBRA. Left cold by other contemporary Dutch paintings.

Cycle out to Scheveningen, a two-pronged fishing harbour. Find a long bustling tourist beach, the mingled rush of water and kids shouting. 'SlagRoomijs' (ice-cream), everywhere friendly flags – for me, the Union Jack.

Back into Den Haag avoiding Madurodam, the miniature Holland park. Head through canals and parks to the Mauritius Huis with its collection of old masters, which leave me cold. In my head there is the enlarged photo of a basket from Vormentaal. But find in a corner a delightful painting of the interior of a church, people standing about nonchalantly looking up, and on the base of a pillar graffitied 'J Houckgeest 1600–61' (1651, Tomb of Willem I, Prince of Orange, in the Nieuwe Kerk of Delft.) A similar one was used by Richard Hamilton in his twinned ancient and modern choice for the National Gallery – Richard Hamilton, *The Sainsbury Wing*, 1999–2000 and Peter Saenredam, *Interior of the Grote Kerk at Haarlem*, 1636–37).

Also enjoyed Vermeer's View of Delft (1660–1), the town seen across the river, the foreground in shadow, the background in sunlight, red tiled roofs, blue water.

    Leon:    This painting later featured in 'Paint it Black: My Research into the Black Plastic as a (self-) portrait in the Cabinet Devriendt', 2015, the PhD of Ghent painter Lucas Devriendt that I supervised.

Toorop (Jan, 1858–1928) cartoons impressed.

    Leon:    though why I cannot now fathom.

Through busy narrow shopping streets to a second-hand book market (can't buy!) I reflect that I have seen little other than the centre. How good it would be to stay in one place! Cap off the day seeing a vast silver-grey Rolls Royce with British pennant flags drift past the Peace Palace. The ambassador? Rule Britannia! The song not the sentiment! At the hostel I converse with a girl from Berlin.

```
DAY 16
THURSDAY MAY 21
DELFT / LEYDEN
```

Through the Hague's standard modern housing fringe to flat uninteresting country...

See spires and chimneys of Delft through heat-haze. Approach along a canal fringed with houses of dramatically different heights. Find the town submerged in dappled light, sun sparkling through trees arching over roads that bridge humpbacked over canals. This is overwhelmingly texture, most are atmosphere, though some houses stand out. I pay 25 cents and climb the spiral stair of the new church spire, and as I climb Delft separates itself from the surrounding country and resolves into a mass of red-orange tiled planes cutting against blue tiles and divided by flashes of leafy light from canals. The town hall, built in the 17th century around a 14th century tower, grows squat. From up here the whole has the anonymity of purpose of an antheap.

> Leon: `I had read Eugene Marais' The Soul of the White Ant at school in Pretoria.`

Man built the means to this view of the glory of god, I have not the faith and find irony in the switched perspective. Down again I visit an 18th century patrician house, darkly comfortable, leather wallpaper, leather upholstered furniture in rooms around a skylit well. Could have hosted salons? I long to sink into an armchair — odd how things so ordinary have become luxuries. Outside I again encounter the striking pattern of humpback bridges. I cycle to an outer canal and watch a barge rising in a lift bridge, soon to go on its hulking way with the stately put-puts of its exhaust. The bank machinery has its ritual: two men turn a swing bridge with a lever. I watch such again and again, gawping like a yokel.

Puncture. Back to the hostel. There with the help of friendly Ernie Verlee...

> Leon: `who I then visited in Amsterdam (Day 30)`

...I fit a new tyre, then walk to a beach, talk to some German girls, and I swim looking far out over the blue-grey sea past a drilling rig towards home. Set off to Leyden with a blonde German girl and two boys, cycling through a wooded belt into which the rich have burrowed.

In Leyden it pours with rain and in my hunger, I buy a pastry which makes it worse. But I end up liking Leyden. It has guts. Where Delft began to cloy, this town has variety; has a humped main street with town hall steps emptied straight into it, leafy canals lined with patrician houses, the view to St. Pieterskerk stands cleft by chestnuts, warehouse houses.

Most of all I am struck by a row of dirty 18th and 19th century stepped gable houses, an alms-house block funnelling out to the clean pink and yellow of the restored facade of the Hooglandsekerk (still spiked with scaffolding), some old, tall warehouses, the classic pillared bridge market, the university – its student life spilling out onto the bridge where I stand, back to the sun, watching the Rappeburg canal.

Out to Kaag rounding a lake, the road winding a little higher than the blue water canal rimmed with yellow-green reeds, and below it, broad meadows stretching to a backdrop of trees, black cattle and a scattering of windmills; cross over on a 'pont', a hand drawn cable ferry, to the Youth Hostel. This, under chestnut trees, is an extension to an old brown brick and shuttered farmhouse. Kaag I realise is an island in a maze of high canals. See in its shipyard the barge Exact, first seen at Dordrecht. The Hostel 'Vader' is very Dutch in his beret and cords. Spend the evening talking to two girls from Munster, liking them.

DAY 17
FRIDAY MAY 22
KEUKENHOF / HAARLEM

Early in the morning cross on the 'pont' and cycle out along a canal high above the meadows, keeping ahead of a barge. Reach uninteresting Lisse where I have a puncture and put in a bigger inner tube. Out through bulb fields but disappointingly I am too late, they are shorn, and men are hoeing, preparing for next season. At Keukenhof I see a blaze of colour under trees, but here too preparation is underway and 'no visitors.' Small farms intensively cultivated seem to pay their way as all have smart cars being Sunday washed.

Through trees to Haarlem. It has the vernacular but is more a shopping centre than an old town. The market square is so cut up by traffic that its form is hard to envision. I make for the Frans Hals Museum and eat a juicy South African Granny Smith on a Dutch canal, leaving only the pips. Ha! Wander into the museum with a group of elderly upper class English tourists and enjoy myself tremendously for three hours. Frans Hals makes me laugh; all those posed faces so nonchalantly unaware of each other's existence . . . fit to purpose but do not sing to me, except for one in which everyone is enveloped in a huge banner. There are miles of followers of Hals paintings, they were onto a good thing! The rooms, tiled waist high, are furnished to period, furniture set out next to the paintings and tables set with cutlery and porcelain of that time. I see French influences. There is a neat chain system for hoisting chandeliers. My favourite room has roman style leather chairs, thick white walls and a rippling cobbled floor. Upstairs there is an exhibition of works by the Post-Impressionist Jan Sluyters (1881–1957). I sit in an armchair, a fine cane one. Leave struck by the huge canvasses by Cornelis van Haarlem (1562–1638). They seem anti-religious. Much celebration of the male form, and a Christ child triptych with two angelic wings and a central slaughter of the innocents: cherubs in anguish, skulls on top of a wheat sheaf, delicately carved timing device from the 17th century pacing the executions . . . Cool comfortable dark rooms, the elegant ticking of Paris gold and white enamel clocks, these stay with me.

See in the Meathall, old documents (printing was pioneered here), photos of the German occupation and an exhibition of the proposed replanning of the market square. A friendly man cycles alongside me, showing the way to the pleasant Jan Gijzen Hostel where I am told that the Dutch Formula One Grand Prix is taking place at Zandvoort. Pass the evening with a yank and two Australian girls. One on one, conversation flowed. Bed late.

DAY 18
SATURDAY MAY 23
BLOEMENDAAL / IJMUIDEN / ZANDVOORT

In morning air through Bloemendaal passing an open-air theatre. I see a huge range of wooded dunes stretching to the horizon in bands of deciduous and non. A new suburb of individually architect designed houses and stagy semi-detacheds set amongst Victorian villas. Cycle to Ijmuiden fishing port. Trawlers are steaming in. A blunt nosed fleet is packed along the quay, repair and trimming in progress. I watch a man paint a ship's bridge white. Men stand about waiting for their pay, sailors already in suits for shore leave. On to Spaarndam where a small metal boy thrusts a small metal hand into a small metal lump of clay. The village sprawls up and down along the dyke. Factories in the distance. Houses are horse-shoed around the lock basin, an island surrounded by boats beyond. A small 'botter' (Dutch side paddle rudder barge) cuts a stream through silky water, rippling reeds along the banks.

    On to the scrubby dunes of Zandvoort. Noise added to noise. Cars, bromfietsen, biplanes advertising Lexington Cigarettes. A wide beach full of people sheltering behind basket weave wind-guards. Watch from the road a practice lap on the circuit. Find it funny, then boring. Cut into a vacation town and see Graham Hill (1929–1975) (I think) stalled in his BRM. Back to hostel riding with the Australian girls on a wooded winding road. Decide to head for Amsterdam the next day.

DAY 19
SUNDAY MAY 24
TO AMSTERDAM

The wind is against me, and so is the traffic. I breathe in fumes, hear only the mosquito whine of the twin strokes, which I dodge. Thousands have this in common: they are on the way to Zandvoort passing me on my way to Amsterdam. I drudge on, following in the slipstream of a man and his wife with a small boy in a wicker basket behind mother. With blocks of flats Amsterdam rises abruptly from flat grasslands. I cycle in thinking to head for the Stedelijk Museum and the Hostel and visit Tante Greta later; but look up and see 'Jan van Galenstraat', turn right then left and find number 101.

    Leon:     This number has dogged me, my RMIT work office number, my apartment number!.

Ring the bell and I am welcomed with a kiss, Tante Greta in her dressing gown, Oom Karel only half dressed. "Oh Leon!" They give me breakfast and we talk. Later I leave for the centre rushing down the road on my lightened bike. Over a canal and a rising bridge and I am at the Dam. Three letters in my pocket, singing joyfully "When it's spring again … tulips from Amsterdam!" Cycle round and round, checking out the hostel (VVV) for later. "Oh, you have a bike!" I head to the Stedelijk, walking quickly through to determine what I will study later. I pedal back more quietly and meet the family, drink beer, "Eet smakelijk!" supper. I ask Tante Greta's pardon and cycle to the hostel and collect the Australian girls and walk them out to a pavement bar and buy them Heinekens to toast me with. I've got my place at the university of Newcastle upon Tyne! Opposite is a church, below is water. It's a bright still evening, we laugh and talk. At last, I point the girls in the right direction and make for 101. Tea and talk until early hours. Oh Amsterdam!

```
DAY 20
MONDAY MAY 25
AMSTERDAM - 1
```

The next morning, after breakfast on gouda cheese, I ride to the Rijksmuseum and see it standing in a park fringed with Victorian villas and see it beyond and through an arched way. It is gargantuan! Inside I find it all too much and too often! No particular painting strikes me. The Frans Hals at Haarlem, seen in domestic space, looked better to me than do these here. Wandering aimlessly, I admire the still lives, set pieces all with knobbled stem goblet and peeled lemon ... Was it a test of translucency? I anchor myself in front of Het Gebed (ca 1656) by Nicholas Maes (1634–1693). I note the way the artist changed the position of the keys hanging from the sill of the nook in the wall. Hue and tone, depth ... this is it! Then I drift until suddenly, from floor to ceiling, I come upon Rembrandt's Night Watch. It's fantastic sucking in of light juxtaposed with darkness has a subtlety that puts Nicholas Maes back in Christmas Card business. Now for me, the Night Watch dominates the entire museum. Though there are Vermeers to come and Pieter de Hooch interiors that put me in mind of Mondriaan's grids. I spend hours amidst the applied arts, noticing mainly – from Zierekzee – a door and panelling incorporating a bed and a fireplace. Also arrays of goblets and stands of church sculptures. I wish the objects and the paintings that depict them were in a more dynamic relationship.

 Struggle on quite sated and head back to the Dam, striking by accident a series of alleys used by pedestrians only, full of shops and crammed with people, and all leading to the Dam. I go happily with the tide, looking at shops and pretty girls, listening to conversations, eating a waffle, admiring the plenitude of sweet and meat displays. The whole stirred by grinding organ music. Fall out into the broad through street near the canal station – all flags and 'rondvaart', buzzing ...

 Make for the Stedelijk museum. Crammed with stuff, but I am now alert to the lack of interaction between objects and paintings. There is an exhibition on Spanish artist and writer Antonio Saura (1930–1998). And of Jaap Mannings which I find pleasant but lacking in force, tension and meaning.

  Leon:  I can find no entry under his name in Wikipedia.

I admire Picasso's Aubergine (1946). The sculpture hall downstairs I find filled with tired metal leafery. Upstairs however I find a totem by Louise Nevelson contrasting with Noguchi's balancing screw and Alexander Calder's black monsters. Many happy moments watching these. Palle

Pernevis's Vissen soon palls, and I find the shapes in Robert Jensen's contrasting squares and rectangles feeble and lacking bite

    Leon:    `I can hear Robin Pitman, our Borlase art master, in my ear here!`

Sit out on the terrace in a basket chair, drinking lemonade, relaxing in the sun and watching across water some blonde Dutch mothers, suntanning one strap at a time, watching their children at play amongst Moores and Rodins. Back out to Jan van Galenstraat where I meet my cousin Arno. Tea and talk till late. Tante Greta and Oom Karel are lively and describe how much they love Amsterdam, how ingrown Zierekzee was.

A warehouse in Amsterdam, with arched window giving light to the office (LvS)

DAY 21
TUESDAY MAY 26
AMSTERDAM – 2

On this, the third morning, I shot the quarter hour into town and into the canals. A beautiful day, light bouncing off windows, skittering off water, rippling down trees and warming my shoulders and back as I lean on a bridge balustrade watching traffic drift by. People are sitting on the steps of their houses. I watch goods being lifted and lowered by beam cranes. I watch across the canal people appearing in openings, a chair and table, a ledge with eggs perched on it, an arched window giving light to an office. Breughalesque. After posting a letter, I reach – as recommended the previous evening – 'Ons Liewe Heer op Solder'. When a wedding ends, I enter. From the outside this is an ordinary merchant house. Inside the top two stories are a church, a double storey volume surrounded by a gallery that is suspended from the roof beams. There is a clear view to an elaborate altar that conceals a slide out pulpit. A guide recounts the history. In the house I note a cupboard bed, the comfortable gloom of the heavily beamed basement kitchen. Cracked tiles and a strong smell of coffee. The curator, hearing of my journey, insists: "Jy moet die Ijsselmeer sien, dit is nou pragtic, hoer!"

    I move on through this web of small canals, trees, old houses, small hotels and bars until through a narrow alleyway I reach De Waag, a fine old fort that dominates its wider canal. The fort screens, flooding over the street, the activity generated by bars, ice cream shops, fruit shops, fish stalls and a hand operated mechanical organ. Inside De Waag there is a fine collection of guild silver. Natural objects, mainly shells are incorporated into the ceremonial flasks. A curtain hangs across an alcove, and looking in, I fall back faced by a giant towering two feet above me! Goliath, glowing red! I recover looking up into the dome, floating calm above galleries. While the dome is encrusted with guild crests, the walls are white. Upstairs I find more silver and open windows in which I sit and watch the street and canal, soaking up the sun. The man grinding the organ pauses to wipe the sweat off his forehead, and to drink (another?) beer. Nearby I enter the Jewish Museum and spend some time realising faintly the horror of the German occupation. How Bucks County Council ordinary the Nazi proclamations appear.

    I go out again into the now drowsy street, and, standing in the shade behind the flower stall, draw it. Then retrace my route wandering through the narrow ways, rising and rolling, often bridged by scaffolding. Tiny shops, houses, blank bare

walls. Pausing, watching, soaking in the sun. Later, round the back of the church I see heavily painted women sunning themselves near their windows. Someone takes a furtive photograph and scrams; but there is no reaction. Bob up eventually in Waterlooplein, and L-shaped square sided by canals and dominated by a renaissance church. This is the flea-market of Amsterdam. I wander through listening to the patter and stirring through the junk: a chamber pot, a television set, books, spanners, scrap iron, clothing, bikes . . . People, some poorly clothed, some eating ice cream, small boys, explore. One old man sits in a quiet corner smashing light bulbs, picks out the elements and pockets them in a fumbling ritual.

DAY 22
WEDNESDAY MAY 27
AMSTERDAM – 3

Rise early and go along the Heerengracht, its stately houses erect on the cobbled quay roadway that waves alongside the canal. Up and over bridges sheltered by tall mature trees. Quietly liveable. There is deep shade down the branch canals. Finally, I pop out onto the banks of the Amstel. Then retreat to the Gracht again, where I stand, back to the sun, watching men lop a tree into a barge. Turning I confront Amsterdam's main contrast: tight nit canals against the dispersed buildings on the wide water of the Amstel. Into the Gracht again, along to the 17th century Willet Holthuysen House. Up steps to wide windows and tall cool rooms, quiet decoration and a small back garden. "Een fles (55) met ingeblazen vertikale strepen (twisted) van melk glas, 17de eeuw, Murano." Classical simplicity. "Rijn wijn glas met te diamant engraveerd" and knobbles on its green glass stem makes me thirsty. A grandfather clock with ships moving on a stationary sea at every tick. Wedgwood vase, brown base, white figures. Two simple inlaid tables, tightly proportioned and well made. A tapestry with an overall flat surface depicting abstracted plant forms, two dogs, a falcon and a man and a woman with their genealogical tables – his and hers. Why did the nineteenth century turn away from this elegant simplicity?

    Through canal streets to Rembrandt's House, well preserved in an area decaying rather depressingly. Spent hours looking at etchings and a few drawings, marvelling at the quality of line, tone, silhouette and contrast of light and dark. "Interior with a winding stair" enthrals. An exhibit of enlarged 'blown up' drawings gave Rembrandt a foothold in abstraction!

    Back in the busy pedestrian shopping network, I go with the tide. Evelyn spoke of orange trees in tubs, and seeing my first, I slip into a quiet pubs and barbers alley and find through a hole in the wall a quiet village square: The Begijnhof. 17th century gabled brick houses face onto grass shaded by a chestnut tree, and on one side a small English Reformed church, cool and white in the sun. Inside are glowing red carpets and memorials. It reminds me of Hedsor Church at home. A house opposite is a Catholic church. This is an Alice Through the Looking Glass moment. Pop out through an arch into rushing shoppers, pop back into rural quiet!

    Down the Prinsengracht to the Stedelijke Museum, where I meet again my Australians! Laugh and chat. I float with pulsing Amsterdam. Back to Jan van Galenstraat for talk in

Maassluis: Inland from Hook of Holland that had been John's point of arrival from England, and close to the field where he spent his first night of Trip64 (JT)

Dutch with Tante Greta and Oom Karel (about income tax!)
Food, tea, biscuits, citrus fruits. "Wel te rusten!"

John: It was my first day of Trip64, as I entered what we used then to call The Continent before the UK joined the EEC on 1st Jan 1973. Not sure how I travelled from Flackwell Heath to Parkeston Quay, Harwich, but it was from there I took the ferry to Hook of Holland. I have always liked Harwich, a much smaller and friendlier port than the Dover I had experienced up until then and Portsmouth which has been the normal route to and fro' between our English and French homes over the last thirty years. I enjoyed Harwich's intimacy and the green route to it through the Essex countryside each time I visited my sister living in Hamburg. I headed to Maassluis on arrival. Looking at pictures of this town as it is now against the two I took, it does not seem to have changed since 1964, although I guess it must have done. Lots of steeply pitched roofs and related valley gutters. Throughout my architectural training and career, I have almost always managed to avoid these gutters which basically exist simply to leak into the building below unless built in a belt and braces way and rigorously maintained. I remember I was very uneasy cycling on that first day - my first two previous trips onto "The Continent" had been in '62 and '63 when my mode of transport had been my thumb, i.e., hitchhiking. There I was cycling through backroads, under power of my legs, on a bike I had built from bits and on roads where people drove on the wrong side. Such was my stress that I ended in a water filled dyke when a cow mooed at me in English! That night I camped out in a field somewhere near Maassluis, but hardly slept as the enormity of what Leon and I had taken on hit me hard - all the way to Rome, you've got to be joking!!!

Fisherman and cyclists sketched along the Ijsselmeer dike (LvS)

DAY 23
THURSDAY MAY 29
TO MARKEN

Ride out to Marken, crossing on the 'gemeente veer' (community ferry) watching the cranes and towers of Amsterdam move to the horizon. Cycle along the Ijsselmeer dike. A hazy hot morning, floating disembodied churches, meadows and meers on the left with cattle and sheep, fishing villages perched on the dike – nets in the water. I climb the dike to see the other side, cross the narrow road link to the island of Marken that looms up above the lake and the mist. Clustered wooden buildings have an air of authenticity but the people in costume look drab and self-similar in the sunlight. No motor traffic, indeed, no roads in the huddled village. May I take your photograph? "Nee. Gaan weg!" (No. Go away!) Puncture...

On through Monnikendam, a pleasant town with windowsills level with the roadway. Find myself quite alone on a small road along a dike dotted with seedy looking holiday shacks. On to Volendam, a modern Dutch town. One or two people in costume, a harbour. Do not stop but bike on to Erian where I have lunch. This town has canals and squares, bridges and alleyways and a clean break with the surrounding country. There is a curiously humped square near the town hall. I am the only tourist. On out to Kwadijk in the heat of the day, humming Mr Heron please don't look at me, I don't like it; don't look at me just like that, I don't want to die Mr. Heron... Progress along a road deep in shade with lush fields stretching away. An avenue now holds the ground, now hovers above it in the haze. Men work bareback on tractors. Farm equipment is moved on flat barges. Puncture. Fix it in the market town of Purmerend. 17th century step gable town hall and the market square divided with cattle pans.

On past Alkmaar along the shipping canal to Schoorl, arriving at 5PM, dead tired. The hostel high in the dunes is full – a girls outing. Sigh, but rally because I know by now that what is unexpected is usually more interesting, and head on out to the Oosterland Hostel with the wind against me. At first this fills me with a nagging anxiety, but soon I regain composure and plod on through the bright sunny evening. The country becomes increasingly wooded and attractive: large fields, the red tiled roofs of barns and farmsteads behind poplar wind screens; fields banded with white and yellow crops. The cycle path is alive and leaps away from the road over canals and through woods beside hedges heavy with blossom, blooms of blue lupins and clumps of rhododendrons,

Rotterdam: Lijnbaan shopping centre with John's bike in sight (JT)

families of wild fowl, ducks on the canal, fine old houses with their thatch cut away in a gable pattern revealing tiles. These are some of the earliest reclaimed polders. Boys swim in a canal that is reflecting the evening glow. A man ferrying his tractor back from the fields to his farmhouse. Looks as if I am going to make it!

 I see the Afsluitdijk and the Ijsselmeer and turn, my back to the wind! The bike trusty and steady free wheels to the village and the hostel, which is thatched, and I am the only guest. The warden is an art teacher. Short talk – it is 8.30 PM! And I am dripping with sweat. Go upstairs. No shower. Improvise one: water out of basin onto me and onto the floor, head under cold tap. Ah . . . Stand drying watching the sun sink red in the North Sea. Catch its last rays across a Friesland herd quietly grazing on the field between the hostel and the water. I stand glowing, thinking of Frank Lloyd Wright and adding tired to tired. To bed.

John:  My second day. Successfully repacked the bike including the heavy damp tent, put my stress behind me and cycled into Rotterdam. After finding the centre of town, as Leon pointed out in his Day 11 piece, I did make a trip to the Lijnbaan shopping centre. I believe Leon's dad an architect of some standing, gave us a list of not-to-miss buildings that might be on or close to our route. The Lijnbaan really was an eye opener and a precursor of things to come - traffic free "streets" with retail, bars, restaurants, etc. either side with their storage on the first floor and projecting coverings making window shopping comfortable in hot or wet weather ... later, of course, leading to enclosed shopping centres or malls. Brent Cross was the first large, enclosed shopping centre to be built in the UK and it set a new standard for destination shopping. When it first opened in 1976, everyone was sure it wouldn't last! I shopped there once it had opened while living nearby in Colindale, North London - the centre being on the North Circular Road around London. Often, I chose purchases in the west end where I worked but bought them in Brent Cross where, surprisingly, the prices were lower.

(above) Delfshaven: Heavy duty barges moored up on a canal (JT)
(below) Delft: Voldersgracht with houses rising out of a canal - just like in Venice (JT)

**DAY 24
FRIDAY MAY 29
ALKMAAR**

Eat an enormous Netherlandish breakfast. Head out to the Afsluitdijk, a fantastic work of engineering. One side the North Sea, the other the Ijsselmeer. Yet, like so much here, undramatic. Sheep graze. Flies buzz. On down to Alkmaar, tired and ambling, quite sure that I will miss the Kaasmarkt (cheese market). And the thought of searching out significant buildings makes me want to drop down on the dike and sleep. Here the cycle path runs along a main canal, linking by locks to low level meadows network. So much is done by water! Milk cans collected, cattle and equipment transported. Some dike repairs underway: a raft of willow wands is sunk against the bank and held in place by a brick and sand infill, and the willow grows.

    Afterall I go to Alkmaar, walking in, wary of punctures. Its Nederlands vernacular, and rounding a corner and there I see, below the clock tower and town hall in a square fronted by shops and a canal, the cheese market. Men in white but wearing coloured hats carry – at a run – sled loads of cheeses. They seem to be keeping time to a rustic band, while dealers thump cheeses and conclude sales by slapping hands, shouting. Huge flat cheeses are loaded onto trolleys and rushed away at a run. Ancient weighing machines. There are pavement pubs on all sides, a bridge in the background. I head back to Amsterdam, planning to sleep at Broek-in-Waterland (Trousers in the water land!) Traverse the housing sprawl of Zaandam, with a weight on my shoulders. A slog. Diagnose a reluctance in me to do more picturesque and change my plan and head back across the community ferry and my spirits rise as the Station and Harbour buildings loom up. Relieved to be again one of many. Cycle to the hostel as Tante Greta and Oom Karel are not expecting me. Find that I can hardly write, my forearms are so stiff. Shower. Walk to De Doelen – a myriad collection of Victoriana elaborates on a junction of canals. Rondvaart boats are mooring, the evening sky reflected in the water. Back at the hostel I sleep fitfully. Did John take the note?

```
John:    What note and from where - presumably this would have
         been about meeting up?
Leon:    So, I also presume.
John:    Day three for me. Enjoyed Delfshaven, a part of
         Rotterdam on the river Nieuwe Maas that goes out to
         sea. Lots of buildings and canals just like Maassluis.
         Set off for Delft. Delfshaven belonged to Delft until
```

Delfshaven: A typical street near an adjacent canal and mixed-use buildings (JT)

1811 when it became a separate municipality and was annexed to Rotterdam in 1886. Got to Delft, presumably without riding on the wrong side of the road for Holland. I really loved Delft but, sadly, have never been back to enjoy its ambience, canals and Dutch buildings.

Delft 64

Delft 64

DAY 25
SATURDAY MAY 30
AMSTERDAM – 4

In the morning I cycle down the Prinsengracht and then spend a quiet morning at Jan van Galenstraat. Gift of cheeses warmly accepted. Talk through my adventures and in the afternoon visit Ernie Verlee in some of Amsterdam's latest housing – pedestrian squares, windy, no gimmicks. Go to the Hostel to see whether John is there. I am looking forward to having someone to share things with but would not have missed having the month alone. Go with Arno and one of his friends by bus and by tram to the Amstel River and see the lines of the Magere Brug against the shimmering water. Back via Rembrandtplein, where under canvas and on the pavement, we drink Amstel beer and watch white bulbs in tubs and trees shaken by wind. Evening people in the streets and daringly (for my companions) we walk through the pink quarter glimpsing one bored prostitute yawning in her window, a man's jacket over a chair in another. Amsterdam is small, I reflect, concentrated in its horseshoe of canals, a family city. I recall a morning near a 17th century wine warehouse with barrels being hauled up on the gable height beam and the sweet smell. Offices all opened onto the street like a doll's house, so often people seem to be bursting out of their houses. Everything goes on in the windows that take up most of the facades.

Spend the rest of the day recuperating, writing up my daybook on the balcony in the sun. I'm not English, not Dutch, nor South African. I am me.

John: My fourth day. I enjoyed Delft a bit longer and drew my first two drawings which were frankly awful ... see opposite. I was not into line drawings particularly during my A-level work at school - mainly painted and sculpted. Realized I would need to improve a lot to avoid being put in the shadows by Leon's work and to keep interested in drawing at all! Determined to get Leon to help me progress. I intend to record any improvement as we travel on. Made my way to Den Haag, a very different place compared with Delft.

The Hague: The Peace Palace (JT)

DAY 26
SUNDAY MAY 31

Reorganise my pack, Go to the Stedelijke in bitterly cold wind. Admire the works of Dutch painter Jaap Wagemaker (1906–1972), in particular a painting using hessian sacking. Traverse the pre-war Dutch surrealism display. Museum fodder. Go to the Weigh House, where I contemplate silver bird closers made for the shutters of a 16th century guild. Accidentally enter the guild chamber marvelling at its carved brick panelling and twisted brick columns. Go to the hostel where I meet John, who is bearded! An evening of talk and wandering. At the pub with orange trees, we have beer, bread and rollmops. In a red-light pub they play Land of Hope and Glory, and we drink Jenever served by a plump barmaid.

John: Last day on my own until the evening. After another cycle around Den Haag went to Amsterdam and met up with Leon at the youth hostel. It really was great to see Leon again, not only to finally get rid of my initial shock of what we had decided to do together, but also to think through sharing the rest of my journey with a like-minded person and my best friend.

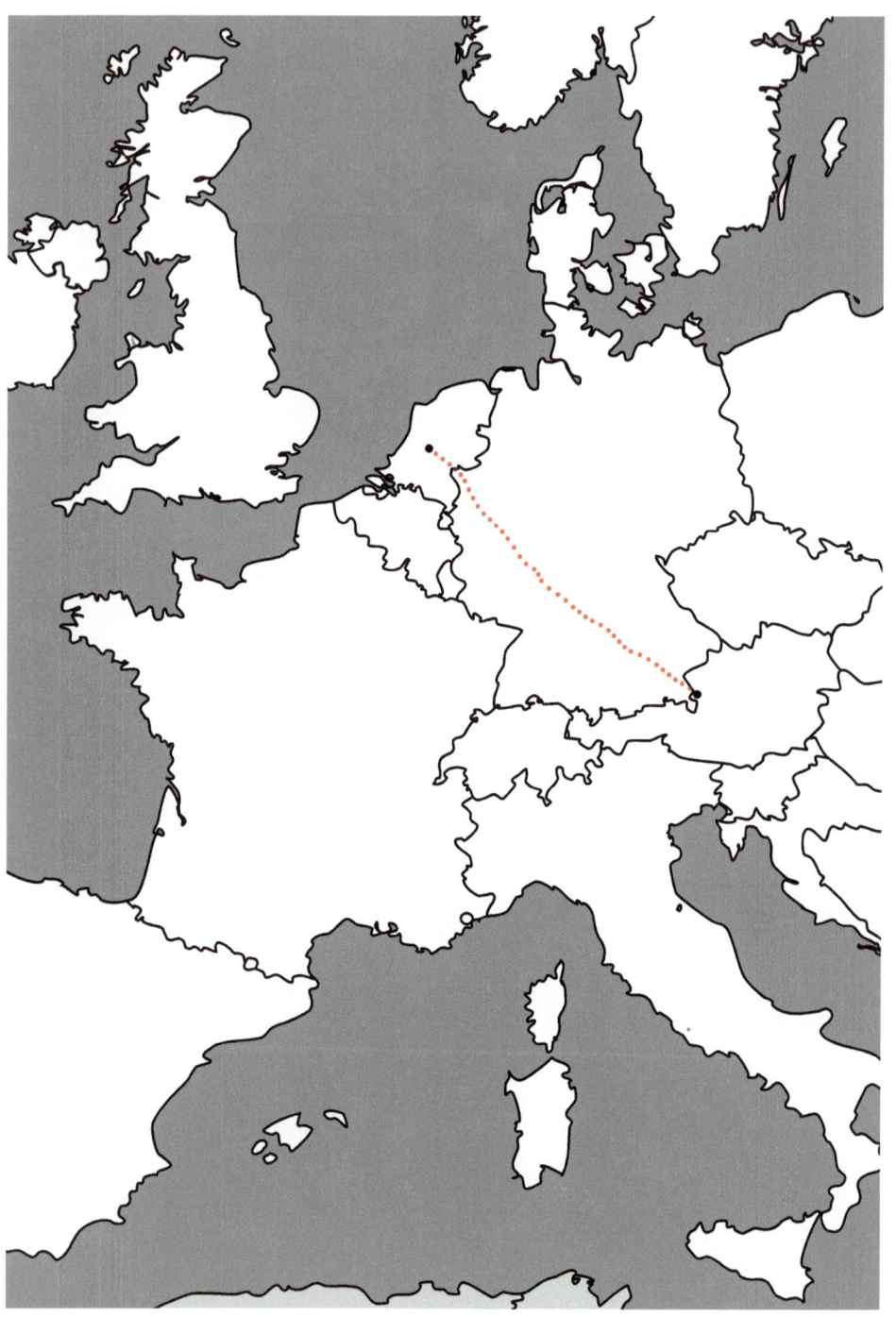

Amsterdam to Salzburg

TIMELINE PART 2 - NETHERLANDS/GERMANY/AUSTRIA

| Day 27 | Amsterdam - 6 | YH Amsterdam |
|---|---|---|
| Day 28 | Amsterdam - 7 | YH Amsterdam |
| Day 29 | Amsterdam - 8 | YH Amsterdam |
| Day 30 | Utrecht / Nijmegen | Leave Amsterdam SE on A2 to Utrecht. Continue SE alongside wooded valley to Rhenen. S to ferry across river Waal. E ghosting the riverbank to centre of Nijmegen. YH Nijmegen |
| Day 31 | Venlo / Border | SSE along A72 to Venlo, ghosting along the border with Germany. SE to border crossing, then E to Hinsbeck. YH full. 1h27 S to YH Hardt. |
| Day 32 | To Cologne | S out of Hardt avoiding Monchengladbach on route 59. Continue SE to Koln. YH Koln |
| Day 33 | Cologne | YH Koln |
| Day 34 | Bonn/ Andrenach / Koblenz | Take the 565 SSE along north bank of the Rhine to Bonn. 1h44. SS along the west bank of the Rhine to Andrenach. 2h25. Seek help at bicycle shop. Follow the south bank of the Rhine to Koblenz, confluence with R Moselle. 1h.11. YH Koblenz |
| Day 35 | St Goar / Bacharach / Mainz | Follow Rhine SSE on route 61 via Boppard, Loreley on the left, Sankt Goar, Bacharach, Bingen. Branch to Rudesheim, cross Rhine to Mainz. 5h12. YH Mainz |
| Day 36 | Worms / Bürstadt / Lorsch / Heidelberg | Follow Rhine S, on route 9 to Worms. Cross river E to Burstadt and Lorsch. Continue E to Heppenheim and take route 3S to Wenheim and Heidelberg. 5.30. YH Heidelberg |
| Day 37 | Heidelberg | YH Heidelberg |

John's cycle pump

| | | |
|---|---|---|
| Day 38 | Neckar valley / Sinsheim / Heilbronn / Schwabisch Hall | Take route 45 E along the Neckar river to Neckargemund, the continue S to Sinsheim. Take route 39 to Heilbronn. Continue via Weinberg E to Schwabisch Hall. 6h32. YH Schwabisch Hall |
| Day 39 | Schwabisch Hall | YH Schwabisch Hall |
| Day 40 | Wasseralfingen / Lausheim / Bopfingen / Harberg (castle) / Donau | SE to Wasseralfingen. Continue E to Laucheim, Bopfingen, and Nordlingen. ESE to Harburg. SSE to Donauworth. 1h.40. YH Donau |
| Day 41 | Donauwörth / Augsburg / Steinach / Munich | S, on Roman Road to Augsburg. Continue SSE to Steinach (Merching). E into Munich. 6h. YH Munich |
| Day 42 | Munich - 1 | YH Munich |
| Day 43 | Munich - 2 | YH Munich |
| Day 44 | To Altenmarkt | E to Altenmark an der Alz. SE to Traunstein. 1h28. YH Traunstein. |
| Day 45 | Traunstein / Salzburg - 1 | E on route 8 to Salzburg. 36m. YH Salzburg |
| Day 46 | Salzburg - 2 | Hugo van Hoffmanstalstrasse |
| Day 47 | Salzburg - 3 | Hugo van Hoffmanstalstrasse |
| Day 48 | Salzburg - 4 | Hugo van Hoffmanstalstrasse |
| Day 49 | Salzburg - 5 | Hugo van Hoffmanstalstrasse |
| Day 50 | Salzburg - 6 - in car to Lake Fuschl / Thalgau / Mondsee / | Hugo van Hoffmanstalstrasse |
| Day 51 | Sunday - 7 - in car / Gaisberg | Hugo van Hoffmanstalstrasse |
| Day 52 | Train to Venice | Train from Salzburg Main Station 7h43m. |

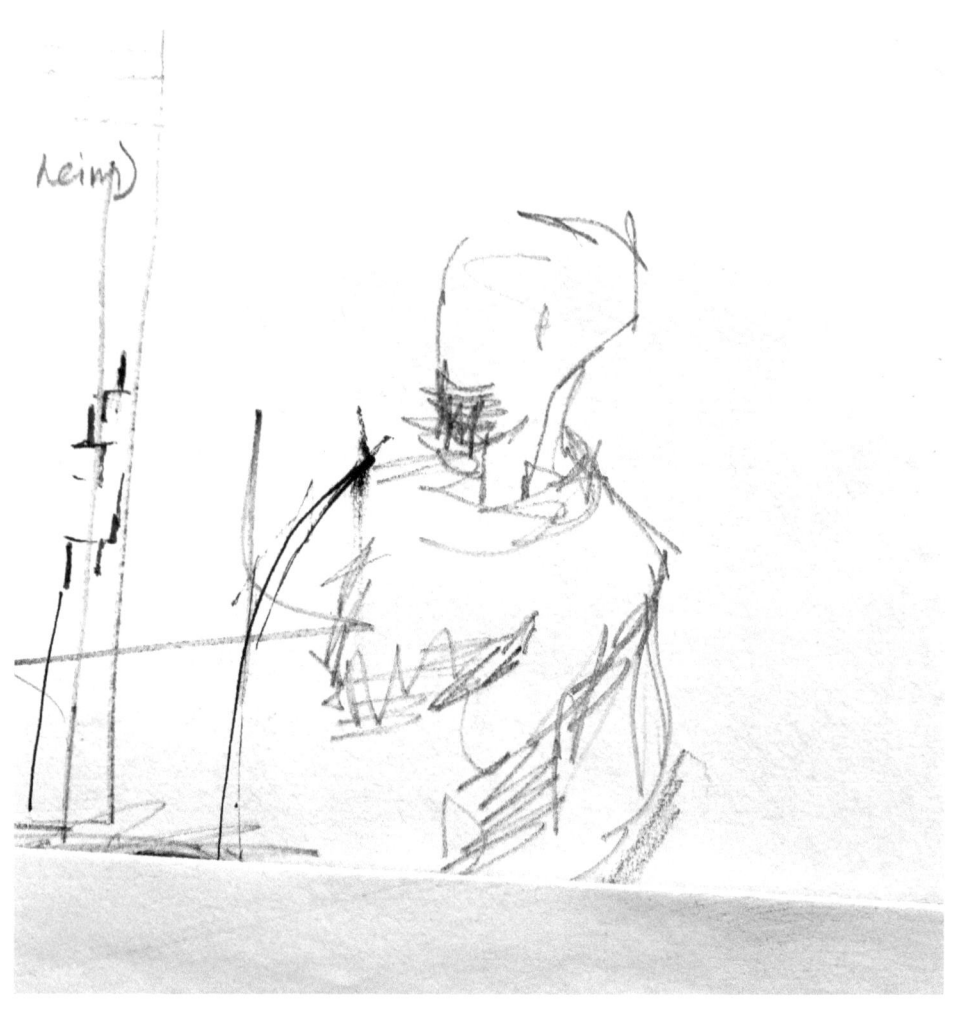

Meet John, who is bearded! (LvS)

## DAY 27 AND DAY 28
## MONDAY JUNE 01 AND TUESDAY JUNE 02

Amsterdam revisited with John: Cold wet day. I revisit, with John, the Rijksmuseum, Stedelijke, wandering through the streets around De Waag. Houses career crazily around corners. We walk through the shopping centre, look into small shops comparing prices, eat patates frites, coated peanuts, rollmops. We go into a pub playing loud early American beat music, drink oude jenever and beer, talk, talk … how I love this city! The wider streets with open sitting on pavements, the narrowing, shop-encrusted alleys, the canals with their patina of old houses. Brick colours, black. The meat shop slogan:

"De Raad van Amsterdam is daarover seker,
Hier kan u beter in gaan as by n apoteker."
(The council of Amsterdam is certain of this, that
It is better for you to enter here than in a pharmacy.)

John: Amsterdam has always impressed me by its apparent open mindedness and simple approach to the basics of modern life. For example, during my first visit in 1962 I was struck by the welcoming attitude ordinary people had towards me as a toffee-nosed English teenager, by my 16 years old head being turned by nice ladies sitting in living room windows overlooking the street … oh, that's why they're sitting there, by their attitude to drinking alcohol, etc.. So different from Londoner's attitude at the time towards "those people from *the continent* … huff", prostitutes selling their wares by jumping out on you from dark corners and "we only drink English gin and beer and Scottish whisky 'ere mate". 10 years later I proposed to and received a positive reply from my then soon to be 1st wife, Vivien, in the back of an Amsterdam cab … not a London cab. Strangely, an almost identical scenario occurred when I proposed to my 2nd wife, Annie, this time in Vienna 20 years later - another country on "*the continent*". Are these differences between the UK and countries on the "*the continent*" a result of the fact that UK was not invaded during either world war whereas most of the countries on "*the continent*" were?

DAY 29
WEDNESDAY JUNE 03

We go to the Heineken Brewery. An incomprehensible tour through bottling machines and between cool fermentation chambers, hot preparation chambers. A myriad of smells, and at last we are treated to cool beer, cheese and mustard. A tremendous view across the watery grey-green jagging of Amsterdam's roofscape, flashes of canals between. Fantastic and I feel joy in my throat that I am here, that Newcastle has worked out, that John is here. Later we take our washing to a laundromat, where we watch it spin and gurgle and get it done with the help of friendly (amused) housewives. In the garden of the Stedelijke, we eat a meal of minty farm bread and carrots. Then walk to the Dam by way of the larger grachts, crossing the hump-backed square, and sit and watch the city from the war memorial. Sit on a bridge over a canal. Tough looking youngsters are doing the same. Rondvaart boats pass under our dangling legs.

    I go to Jan van Galenstraat to say goodbye. (Did John come too?) We drink bessenjenever, talk. We have a meal of egg salad and spaghetti. I have grown very attached to them. Over washing up, Oom Karel says proudly of immaculately coiffed and corseted Tante Greta (she must be 80 years old): "Van agter Lyceum, van voor Museum!" (from behind Lyceum, from the front Museum). "You must come again! We have talked so much that I now have eleven English words! Arno joins us. I give Tante Greta a gift of chocolate biscuits and tea. We all kiss goodbye. "Next time bring your wife!" says Oom Karel winking. (I did not see them again, but we corresponded through my father's older sister who, when she visited us in London a few years later, visited them.)

John:     I don't recall going with you to your aunt's place ... missed some of the fun and food.
Leon:     Not sure why, but I went alone. She was my great aunt, already in her 80's. Maybe that's why.

DAY 30
THURSDAY JUNE 04
UTRECHT / RHENEN / DE WAAL / NIJMEGEN

This day is a flash of impressions. Leaving Amsterdam by the wider business district streets we cycle through flat open country, then — before Utrecht — turn off onto winding brick-paved roads through a wooded area. Fine old houses are set primly over ponds with lawns coming to the edge of the road. We come to a small canal and an old brick castle in a style reminiscent of de Waag. Then rush into Utrecht along a canal bank. Have a cool beer in the cool inn where I asked for water to fix my puncture, and the innkeeper almost does this for me. An old man smoking a giant cigar joins the talk. "Kom weer wanneer uw terugkom!" (Come again when you return. There was no return.) We leave Utrecht glimpsing the tangled medieval centre between Victorian villas.

Take a wooded road to Rhenen, trying to freewheel down the first hill that I have encountered in the month! But the wind holds me back, and I have another puncture. Cadging water elicits more help and more chatting in pidgin Dutch. We sit, eating our packed supper on the raised approach to a bridge, Rhenen straggling red over its hill, barges put-putting away below and the spire standing away from the hill, emphasises it. We take the ferry across de Waal, spanking neat with the captain's bridge to one side. The conductor is of Indian origin. Feel evening settling, smell the coolth of the water as it is churned by the propellers.

Nijmegen, straggling between river and hill, has neat modern houses, a concrete hall. People (who may as well be in a vacuum flask) are assembling for a — to me — disembodied ritual. We swoop down to the Hostel in a valley, the sun setting against the bridge and over trees. Through the arched window of the vaulted dormitory, watch the light dancing through the evening, isolating spires in pockets of light and shade, looking miles over flat land. Sleep till the sun reaches my bed under the open window.

DAY 31
FRIDAY JUNE 05
VENLO / BORDER WITH GERMANY / HINSBECK / HARDT

Down to Venlo in a gale. Tired. Mesmeric play of uprights: avenue against stands of corn, against canes for hops. Cherry trees are speckled red and scarecrows are thrust out. Germany is high on the left. Freewheel in cooling showers, Germany on our minds. Amsterdam was a climax. Shop in Venlo for bread and head to the border, the wind with us. Subtle change to landscape after border – it no longer looks as if it has been made, and villages have 'just happened' look. The wind is gusty, and John's eye is scratched. We find the handsome hostel at Hinsbeck is full and press on to Hardt where the deeply-eaved hostel is in a wood, where we are given our own room. Sleep well.

(above) Cologne: Evening train passing the cathedral and over the Rhine (JT in 1962)
(below) Cologne: Similar position showing the "dramatic juxtaposition" (JT in 1962)

DAY 32
SATURDAY JUNE 06
KOLN / COLOGNE

To Koln (as the signs have it), passing the HQ of the British Army of the Rhine. Wooded country becomes rolling and has its own kind of monotony. Pylons. Pylons. Glimpses of villages shrouded in trees. Noise! Roaring, shaking of motor traffic. The dead straight rise and fall of the Roman road. On every rise we see the twin towers of the cathedral. Reach the bedraggled outskirts, tired trees wilting under the onslaught of sun and traffic. Dingy fruit stalls. Vicious cobbles. Eventually the buzz of pedestrians, the rebuilt shopping centre. Geometric blocks. A glimpse of the cathedral. Linked squares lined with tubs of flowers between glass buildings. Pause under an awning, catch a glimpse of people against grass, and looking up in the gap see the pile of the cathedral. The spires, seemingly solid from a distance, are honeycombed! I can see the sky through them! The cathedral should soar, yet it squats – a magnificent pile like pile that forces every piled block into prominence. It staggers up in rising weight. Inside, one lesser volume emphasises a larger. Still the weight presses. Evening sun pierces the made-black west end. There is a moving vista of pouring sun through the pillars. Candles are lit in blazing coffin-like trays. The Red Prelate herds us out. In mist and rain the cathedral is isolated in a haze of sunlight. A railway bridge humps in contrast and in heavy sympathy. "In Germany it is not the custom to sit on the grass!" Two full length leather coated, peaked capped policemen interrupt our reverie. We move to a bench and read The Observer as the crushing thrust of the cathedral is made to fall by the passing clouds.

John: The Observer is published on Sundays in UK and one is lucky to get one in some parts of continental Europe by Monday night. I remember the paper reading, strangely enough, but was it the previous Sunday's issue?

Leon: We bought it massively discounted because out of date. Way beyond our budget on Sunday!

John: I felt at home when I arrived in Koln - my 3rd visit there. My first sight in 1962 of the verticality of the stone 13th century twin towered cathedral reaching for the sky against the powerful horizontal spans of the post-WW2 steel railway bridge reaching across the Rhine, knocked me sideways by their dramatic juxtaposition. The same happened again as I turned up in 1964, this time with Leon. Neither the cathedral nor the pre-WW1 bridge were badly damaged by the Allies in WW2, but the bridge was destroyed by the

Cologne: The classic German 60's Youth Hostel we stayed in
(JT in 1962)

Leon: Germans on their retreat to Berlin at the end of the war, like many others over the Rhine. The bridge was re-built much in its original form soon after the war followed by subsequent adjustments. Near the eastern end of the bridge was the youth hostel in a quiet zone and on the western end lots of fun to be had including at riverside hostelries, the two perfectly linked by an easy walk over the bridge and past the cathedral – what could be better?

Leon: the towers are a nineteenth century Gothic revival addition, not less amazing for that!

**Modern Hostel, very regimented. Rules pasted up. Spend the evening in an old inn on The Rhine. Drink beer in pottery mugs. It goes to my head. Fat waitress. Locals. Leberwurst and kartoffel salat. Through the door the river and a monolith glinting. The scrubbed smooth white tables invite fingering. Two eggs, ham, fried toast and Bitburger Pils. The hum of conversation. Laughter. The pinched face of the bar-lady who then smiles at me. Leaded windows. The woman eating scrambled eggs and chips, double chin, polka dot dress and fringe cut hair. Flow of greetings as people move in and out. The navy-blue lady's chicken-laugh. The stagger to the door.**

John: Our first evening in Koln was spent in the same inn I first visited in 1962. I remember well the crushing realisation then that here in Germany you could eat as well as drink in pubs. Something that had yet to arrive back home. At that first visit I ate with the friend I was travelling with Heißes Wurstchen und Kartaffel Salat and loved it so I repeated it this time. Sitting on the benches along the back wall of the inn we drank and ate, looked at the barmaid and out towards the Rhine and got excited all again about our journey still to be experienced.

Cologne: "barges struggle up" the Rhine (JT in 1962)

DAY 33
SUNDAY JUNE 07
KOLN / COLOGNE

Walk through shops with Sunday window-gazers, comparing prices. The neon sign of a Japanese restaurant flickers dimly. The older town: Bullet holes in the walls, the questions crowd in. Why? How? Did you help Jews? What did you do? But I don't ask. We go to a concert in a new hall joined to the ruins of an old one by glass walls. No one coughs. No one moves. What did these comfortable burgers do? A diva comes onto the stage and sits impassively until just before the concert ends, when she rises and shrieks. Thunderous applause. What are 20 years? Have they chipped away the horror to nothing now? How can I know? Will it happen again?

We walk in the sunshine on the edge of the rushing, bridged Rhine. Flats point the distance, barges struggle up, swift down. On the far bank there is a tent, no structure visible from here. A dishcloth thrown and caught in flight; it is taut. We marvel at the contrast with the piled heaviness of the cathedral. In daylight the upper surfaces dominate. At night dance music drifts across the water and the under surfaces are lit.

Back at the hostel – a well-constructed bunker – the architecture echoes with Nazi boots, but the bomb sites we see also echo...

John: Unlike Leon I did enjoy the youth hostel, not just to be different, but since I had been there before I could ignore its negative aspects. I just enjoyed the silly bits. Unlike many other hostels, you were given a linen bag to get into on your bunk, which you returned on departure for cleaning and recycling. To go on top of that you were given a blanket which had the word Fußende (Foot End) printed big. In the morning you were not allowed to leave until your folding of the blanket had been approved with Fußende showing on top. Having achieved release from the dorm, it was down to the minimal breakfast served with Ersatzkaffee and shared with nice brown legged jolly girls.

(above) Beside the Rhine close to the location of the "first temper tantrum" (JT in 1962)
(below) Koblenz: The confluence of the Moselle with the Rhine (JT)

DAY 34
MONDAY JUNE 08
BONN / ANDRENACH / KOBLENZ

Our ride to Bonn is through unremarkable industrial landscapes. We are blown up-river by the wind. Bonn is mellow. Cycle through narrow streets to a square with a flower market. Plaster and paint pointed neo-classical buildings and Romanesque church, round arches inside. Parks, modern shops, an avenue to a big house. Out into sprawl, and I look up and here is the first pointer to the Rhine gorge – a towering spur with the remains of a castle perched on it.

Freewheeling down to the river, my tyre shreds. In Andrenach, the village at the base of the hill, there is a cycle shop in a twisting old street. The proprietor shakes his head. "Your wheel is not metric!" His wife shows with pride their daughter's English exercise book. Proprietor puzzles on how to help me. "Wait a minute! Before the war my father stocked spares for English tourists!" He rummages at the back of the shop and finds: "De Engelse ding!" A white tyre that fits.

Leon: At least 30 years old, it gets me to Rome!

John: Whether it was Day 34 it happened or during the next couple of days before we crossed the Rhine after Worms to head east, and whether it was as a result of the wind behind us or Leon's shredded tyre going down to Andrenach, I will never know. When, where or why it occurred doesn't really matter, but our first temper tantrum kicked off. I was pleasuring in the passing images of the Rhine and its banks when I suddenly realised Leon was not behind me. I stopped immediately and waited for some time and eventually spotted him coming around a bend in the river way down stream. When he reached me there was a torrent of expletives heading my way. What he said I can only guess but his vehemence was so extreme I automatically responded with words to the effect " ... if you don't bloody keep up we'll never get to Rome ... ". It was quite unfair on my part to respond like that – all the things we had only one of such as the central map collection, the tent, bike mending knowhow (in my head and tools), etc. were all on my bike. Needless to say we forgave each other over a couple of beers later on.

All the way to Koblenz the sides of the valley close in. We find the town drab and grey. It bridges the Rhine and the Moselle junction.

John: As soon as I saw the confluence of the Rhine and Moselle, I thought of my dear dad in 1937 being pot shotted at during his canoeing trip on the Moselle

Koblenz: The Rhine looked down upon from the Youth Hostel (JT)

when he (perhaps inadvertently) wound up the Germans on the banks by having a Union Flag pennant on the bows of his canoe.

We rise up through the huddle, to a fort on an immense cliff. It's the Hostel. We secure our places. Drag our bikes up through arches between trees, the town receding, the Rhine widening into an agonising reflection of the evening sun. At the top we reach a courtyard with Palladian facades through the arches in which we see a sheer drop to the river. The huddle of the medieval city contrasts strongly with the precise geometry of modern blocks, all slung between the two rivers.

Leon: Later, studying at the Architectural Association School of Architecture in 1970, I would be introduced to Colin Rowe's figure grounds by David Grahame Shane. One of Mainz revealed just such a contrast.

We eat Mars Bars!!

Leon: These were made in Slough where I had worked to earn the money for this trip.

Talk to an American from Florida who "is always on the hop!" He looks for "the seamy side" wherever he goes. There is a Swede who is studying medicine. The Hostel is drafty and cold. I catch a chill. Our meal is pumpernickel, Sausage, raisins, biscuits, orange chocolate and milk.

Bacharach: Vernacular timber framed lath and plaster buildings. (JT)

DAY 35
TUESDAY JUNE 09
BOPPARD / ST GOAR / LORELEY / BACHARACH / MAINZ

We leave the hazy town sent off by ornate and decayed plasterwork on an isolated row of pre-war houses. Coast a long bend of the Rhine, Vineyards on the sunny side North of the river, bush on the South. See, above the huddle of St Goar, the church – twin-towered and thrust against the valley wall. Small, ruined castles ride the valley tops; the flanks are combed into lines of arid growth, terraced with brick retaining walls to keep soil for vine roots. A cliff on a bend turns out to be Loreley. Boats, pleasure steamers, cruisers, barges. A castle on an island with bulbous turret domes. Flash through St Goar, a glimpse down an alley to a high orange wall, one arched opening, two dark trees, and the flash of the Rhine beyond. An alley, a nun walking black past, a tree filling a small square. Crazy angles of ancient timber, plaster and lath construction.

John: The normal description in Europe is "lath and plaster" construction – the laths are nailed on first to the structural timber and then the plaster is applied to the laths including the gaps between them.

But the thunder of traffic dominates.

Boppard is cut off from the river by road and rail. Through a half-timbered archway we find a baker, greengrocer and a post office.

John: Maybe this is where the heavy tent on my bike was posted home.

Uphill, above the pink ruin of a church we find a leafy courtyard, a wooden spiral staircase twisting up into a second floor.

Hot slog into Mainz through patch crop country, heavy traffic, valley side misty in the distance. The Hostel, above the river on the seedy side, is modern. Shower. Laze. Fab group of girls. Fine hostel meal. In the evening sun we all sit on the porch and sing, always Anglo-American sounds. A boy has an electric guitar and plays only one song: "I got the hippy hippy shake." (Hippy, Hippy Shake by The Swinging Blue Jeans, a four-piece Merseybeat band, 1963.)

Just relax. Those girls! Think of home.

Heppenheim: "circular tree seat in the shade ... Kendal mint cake". (JT)

DAY 36
WEDNESDAY JUNE 10
WORMS / BURSTADT / LORSCH / HEPPENHEIM / WEINHEIM / HEIDELBERG

Straight out to Worms through rolling peppercorn combed vines, then berry fruit and corn strips, with the occasional worker. Worms is hot, dusty industrial on the Rhine, with a few quiet shady Victorian residential streets, a green park in an old moat, a tired shopping district. We approach the cathedral up steps, see it through an arch in an ivy clad wall. It's a great pink lump defaced by restoration work in progress. A touch of the Roman in the arches. Enter through a side door – immense gloom, thick pillars, one beam of sunlight falling into the body of the nave from a window behind the dome arch, disembodied and hazy as from heaven. Mystery and superstition. Candles in one corner under spot lit pink hydrangeas. Imagine a midnight mass, lit only by candles. Gloomy dark baroque altar and bits in the altar alcove. That beam of light. A magnificent tool for domination.

We buy provisions and wine! Cycle towards Burstadt

John:      Crossed the Rhine for the last time.

The approach is fabulous, the tiled onion turrets of the church above huddled houses against Rhine valley ridges hazy in the distance. Lorsch is 1200 years old. Half-timbered, pink and white panelled houses lean in 'Y's against each other. A little chapel behind a tall arched gate on a hill above the village centre. A tractor chugs out, drawing a trailer. Two brown and brawny farmer wives sitting in it, greyish floral dresses, hair drawn back, they hold paper parcels of food.

Leon:      In her enthralling book "Stealing from the Saracens"
           (Hurst and Company, 2020) Diana Darke explains how a
           "highly influential printed map of Jerusalem (Mainz,
           1486) wrongly shows the Dome of the Rock sporting an
           onion dome." The Crusaders had (wrongly) believed that
           this was a Christian shrine. The map was continually
           reprinted into the mid eighteenth century. Onion
           domes became fashionable in the west in the sixteenth
           century, a fashion that persisted in "the rural
           architecture of village churches in the Alps."
           (pp 125-6)

Straight road through woods contrasts with the hot dry strip farms. Heppenheim is tucked against the Rhine valley wall. We sit on a circular tree seat in the shade, bikes against an old pump, sucking Kendal mint cake. Shops and garages to the side, in front a white and brown timbered row, a road moving higgledy away and turning oblique above the green flank of the valley. And one tower.

Tiled onion turret of the church at Burstadt (LvS)

Road now rolls along the bottoms of hills; they are covered with crops and vines. At Weinheim we stop and ask for water, buy German pastries, sit under the "Trink Coca-Cola" sunshade and talk in pidgin and hand signs to an old man about university, beer (he is drinking from a tankard) and about the war (his topic). We tell him that we are cycling to Rome. "English youth is adventurous. Maybe that is why we lost the war..." The pastries are flaky with sugar and treacle. The road to Heidelberg is hotter and dustier, passing the Mannheim industrial sprawl. At roadwork traffic lights we chat with people who think we are Dutch.

We reach the hostel and sit in the shade until 5.30 PM. The heat is oppressive. I am reminded of South Africa, the difficulty of moving after 12 o'clock. Here as there, school is over at 1.30 PM. There are three huge South Africans here, wearing pyjamas and clothes such as I used to wear. Our meal: speckled sausage, rye bread, two oranges and a litre of cheap Rhine wine – Oppenheimer Kurtenbrunner 1963, tangy and yellow – and before we know it, we are under the table. We'd smuggled the bottle onto the terrace as a non-alcoholic beverage... Staggered out, trying to hide the bottle, singing! Walked to the tucked-into-the-hill bridge over the Neckar, still singing. The old buildings glowing pink and on the river a barge and two racing dinghies. Decide to stay here the next day. Back slightly sober.

Heidelberg: Leon having a beer away from the sun (JT)

## DAY 37
## THURSDAY JUNE 11
## HEIDELBERG

Early up to the schloss, heat weak. Over the bridge, along a shopping street with the cool greenery of the Rhine wall climbing on the right. Buildings plastered orange, classical motifs. Slowly we struggle up steep alleyways hunting the shade, relishing the cool damp recesses in the walls on one side, the cool rooms of houses on the other, winding up and up while the work of the day goes on: printing, students leaving their lodgings, tourist traps opening and spreading brightly coloured lures. Steps now, and the pink stone of crumbling battlement hang in shade above. Sit and look into the valley. Most of the villas climbing the hills are Victorian but drawn very distinctly from a schloss-Bavarian-alpine mould. English gothic whimsy is quite different in atmosphere.

At last, up over a deep ditch chasm and through a tunnel, and there is a mansion – carvings around its windows, a blend of ancient stonework and 17th and 18th century classical. A fountain, the sound of water, sit in the shade. Can I hold this all? Can I remember every second? The camera is impotent. Out through trees to a view over the Neckar. We have a beer outside in the shade. Delicious! But still the straining agony of wanting it all, always.

Down into the town. Sit again, on other steps. Wander into shopping streets, out to a tree on the river, watch barges queuing for the lock under a lovely arched bridge. Buy apple pastries. Walk out into the main square, where a screened building shows up the glories of the surrounding plasterwork facades. One of which with its reddish earth plaster and precisely shaped details, I watch. Sit in a park eating juicy local cherries, footsore across a bridge, sit underneath chestnuts watching people buying ice cream from a lady with a canopied tub. People are swimming in the river, sunbathing on the bank; people are watching me watching them and the town across the way. It all fits into place. I can't hold it, I can share it, enjoy it, live it, leave it. Holding on kills the enjoyment.

Sitting and walking back to the hostel, I reflect again on the South African feel – boys going home from school through the heat of the middle of the day. At the hostel, sleep a bit, hungry and tired. Decide not eating well enough – we had no lunch. Our evening meal: speckled sausage, rye bread, cabbage, peanuts, cherries, apples, milk. Early to bed after talking with a much-travelled Australian and a cramped American Honda enthusiast.

(above) Schwabisch Hall: Wooden bridge over the river and giant warehouse beyond (JT)
(below) Schwabisch Hall: Buildings overlooking the river (JT)

## DAY 38
### FRIDAY JUNE 12
NECKARGEMÜND / SINSHEIM / HEILBRONN / WEINBERG / SCHWÄBISCH HALL

Up the Neckar between villa hills to Neckargemund, then into the hills towards Singheim. The country is attractively wooded. "Umleitung" diverts us through small lanes, fields and trees, along a stream under trees, past an old barn and a house stretching tiled across the head of the tiny valley. Out the other side we walk our bikes up the hill. There are rolling fields of corn, a row of workers, ranges of trees. There is birdsong. It is fabulous. The Rhine was never quiet; spectacular but never as dramatic as it had pretensions to be, always a bit anticlimactic. But here on the smaller scale everything works. Trees along the road, villages unashamedly scruffy. Crumbling white barns, their yards filing the air with the smell of cattle and produce. Glimpses of inner courtyards, the debris and odds and ends of ages. Then we are out again along the winding road, level wheat on both sides glistening in the sun, cut off by the shade of a wooded hill and a line of poplars. Pools of shade where umbrella apple trees are suspended over the wheat.

Later, the road is straight and unremitting, but the country still holds fun. In one village we shelter from the beating sun in a Gasthof lounge, drinking Coca Cola amidst yellow panelling and talking to the daughter of the house. Struggle on through sticky tar and pleasant enough country to Heilbron, where we have a meal at a modern hostel, but the town we leave behind and head to Weinberg, cleaving the heat. From here to Schwabisch Hall, I had a longing for others to see what I was seeing. A countryside that made me want to cheer; that made me sing 'Trink, trink. Trink!" and wave my arms about. Everything worked in with everything else. All the narrowness that I felt in Germany up to now was gone. Here, on sun-browned earth, grapes ride the hills in patches, right around the Weinberg wine hill. Greenery, earth, earthy green. Trees crown the hills. The people work the fields ruddy and bronzed, and then grow fat on the produce: wine, beer, bread and sausage. A large red farm cluster tops its vineyards, A town crests the highest ridge, and we rise up to it by hairpins. Haymaking is going on, screened sometimes by trees. Fields are punctuated with yellow stooks, trees and fields. Fields flow into valleys, to the edge of cliffs. The sun weights all. Great patches of shade soothe from the woods.

From the town there is a view of dotted patches of vineyards running to a horizon of rolling ridges. On the tops rolling wheat land cuts into shady forest. On, on through this country, so much itself and knowing that, as do

Schwabisch Hall: Alley with tin plate sign "Frisseur" (LvS)

Northamptonshire fields, Cornish Cliffs and Game Pass, the mountain lodge of my childhood summers.

Stop. Salt has crystallised on my forehead. Drink a litre of water and a coke and head on down into another river valley, the bikes rolling quietly. An anti-climax. A small village, extreme humid heat, think only about the hostel. Where can Schwabisch Hall be? Suddenly we drop into the river gorge and there it is! Piled crazily into the narrow chasm, tiled roof cutting over tiled roof, half-timbered front over half-timbered front, up to the flanks of a giant warehouse. Down across the sparkling river and in! Up narrow alleyways each cut into by jutting upper storeys. Inner courtyards, baroque decorations. The town square rises up to the church, flanked by steps. We look back: there is a baroque orange town hall, stepped gable houses along each side of a square. It's too rich to take in. Up one alley there is the tin plate sign of a "friseur". Pink upper storeys lean together, there are houses in courtyards beyond. A cat plays in the shade. Round a corner we confront the giant gable of the Warehouse. Tucked in beside it is an ancient tower and a medieval half-timbered building – the hostel! We are the only guests, but a student is lodging there. An old hausfrau is in charge. We park the bikes and wander out to the river. Look up again to the thrusting geometry of the roofs leading up to the dominating triangle of the warehouse. We cross over the old wooden bridge with its thick beams supporting its tiled roof. The tower at one end is still used as a house! An alleyway funnels away bridged by a two-way balcony. Intricately wrought iron signs. We dine on Lowenbrau and wurst, alongside labourers old and young, in the cheapest pub. A marvellous day! We must stay to see some more. Will we ever get to Munich?

John: Just like Leon I relished our arrival in Schwabisch Hall. This was the Germany I had missed on my two earlier hitchhiking trips to Italy when main traffic routes were all important and I was delighted to find it here. Much of what we had experienced so far in Germany was on the Rhine, areas badly affected by WW2 bombing and the post-war recovery. Schwabisch Hall, although bombed a couple of times towards the end of the war, had survived well. It was a real medieval town. My only two Trip64 drawings done so far were of Delft, but Schwabisch Hall forced out the drawing pad and pens again for the next two. Drawing in a medium I was unused to, what I did in Delft was pretty dire but, with guidance and confidence given me by Leon the next two seemed to be moving in the right direction.

Schwabisch Hall: giant warehouse that houses the Youth Hostel (LvS)

DAY 39
SATURDAY JUNE 13
SCHWABISCH HALL

Early in the morning, before the heat, we go down past half-timbered houses on the left of the church. Past the baroque town hall, a vegetables market is in session under coloured umbrellas. We find a supermarket where we hunt for our needs amongst stacks of tantalizing goods: sardines, cheese, soap, milk and treacle. Out to the riverbank and sitting on a sloping ledge on top of the old town wall, under chestnut trees, we eat our breakfast: thick pumpernickel and treacle, milk and sweets. Discover that the cheese we could afford, a dark beige block, is inedible. Is it even cheese? We sit drawing the buildings across the river. We have settled in a meeting place. Old women with baskets of purchases from the market, scarves over their hair pulled into buns, over wrinkled brown faces, over faded floral frocks. They nibble and chat while waiting for buses. Old men with sloppy moustaches and sticks come later. Then little boys. Boats are rowed on the dammed river, their reflections split at the weir. We wander on along the bank, looking, prying, as if in a plum pudding. Too much! Steps dark between houses, which clog together. Above us is the sunlit flank of the warehouse. Builders at work on a house have put bottles of beer in a fountain. A tower appears above the houses. The sun as it moves changes everything. We pass through a small pastel courtyard, a cool alley and reach the town square. Go out into it and up to the church, where we sit on the steps and watch the jostling of roofs.

John: Our eating habits during Trip64, was for subsequent years, the source for many a shaggy dog story. One of these grew out of our stay in Schwabisch Hall. It goes something like this " ... cor, you were lucky! Well, before starting at university, thanks to my taking A-levels a year early and getting a place at Sheffield University School of Architecture ... yes, I went on an amazing cycle trip with my best mate from home to Rome ... yes all that way! We had very little money and therefore could not eat very much. I remember endless meals of pumpernickel and black treacle. At some place in the middle of Germany I found some really cheap cheese in a little supermarket, cheap I thought because it was locally made, which neither of us could eat because it was awful. I subsequently found out that it was in fact furniture polish ... yes, furniture polish!"

Leon: I well remember trying to eat that 'cheese'!

Schwabisch Hall: The narrow streets, drawn and photographed (JT)

Down to the river for our lunch, a repeat of breakfast. All has changed with the changing shadows. Back up to the town centre, in foot leadening heat. We dwell on the decoration of the houses: here a chair carved into buttresses, there intricate leaf wrought iron, here baroque fun in pink and gold. We shelter from the thick heat in the hostel, going up the brown wooden steps stretching from cool white wall to cool white wall to the dormitory. Note the intricate lock mechanism of the door with curling handles, wrought iron plates in the shape of persons, honey coloured wood, the coolth within. Sleep.

    In the late afternoon we go out to the island in the river below. It is being prepared for the Sommernachtsfest. Benches being arranged in ranks under the trees, red and yellow lanterns and flares being set up. Committee men bustle about checking. The bratwurst stalls of a fair are already operating. We sit on the bridge which is exuding warmth – now welcome! – from its day in the sun. A blind man plays the accordion and watches girls legs go by. We eat supper in the pub again: Hellbeer, tages, suppe, bratkartoffel and bratwurst. People drink and wait for darkness. Buxom barmaid flirts with everyone. We go out, full. And our eyelids are dropping. At the tower hostel we wash in the alcove high up. Wrought iron balustrade and white troughs, and a view over the town. Fall into bed and sleep. Fireworks crash like a drunk coming up all those steps! The fireworks give way to a thunderstorm as the weather breaks. A fabulous day, so much and so little our capacity to describe it!

Nordlingen: Approach to town (above LvS / below JT)

### DAY 40
SUNDAY JUNE 14
WASSERALFINGEN / LAUCHHEIM / BOPFINGEN / NÖRDLINGEN / HARBURG / DONAUWÖRTH

Push our bikes up out of the chasm early in the morning. The lighting today is more subtle. There are moving clouds and patches of sunlight. We breakfast under an apple tree: vollkornbrot and treacle. All morning we follow the river valley, the scenery quieter. A moulded rivulet flows along the valley walls. The way is dotted with orchards and there are individual fruit trees scattered along the road. Light green cropped grass runs smoothly up to deep hanging conifer shade at the hill tops. The road bends, following contours; now above the cutting winding stream with lush reed banks where it recedes. Now alongside rapids, now through fields where Sunday means that the last of the hay must in! and all of the family turn it to air it after the rain. Up into a village, with church bells pealing quietly over the still, unhurried valley. People walk up to the church wearing black, faded florals. Young girls walk quietly, bibles in hand. Textures change in the opening, unfolding and disappearing valley inlets; grass now mown lawn-like under apple trees, now fields bounded by the river and the road roughage are mown clean, old lace and flashes of red poppies, fields with hay stacked on triangle treadles, hay lying in stripes, hay rumpled unevenly... And overall, the smells of animals, of rapids, of damp woods.

John:   More pumpernickel and black treacle!

We sweep by fishermen on the banks, through white gabled and red tiled villages. The winding and gouging stream reminds me of the grass lined river valleys of Game Pass in the Drakensberg krantzes. We stop for a coke in a Gasthof just above the river. It has an old yellow yield entrance lobby, worn wooden stairs, rough plastered walls, one small table, dark doors, a bronze plaque commemorating the Zeppelin and plumbing of the same date with tin basin and tap under mirror and a worn spot in the floor. There is a barred gate silhouetted against the light at the top of the stairs. A rough country woman is brushing down the stairs. There are fine horses in a stable on the same floor.

Wasseralfingen brings change: a wide rolling country and differently made villages. Lauchheim is built of golden stone – no plaster. Bopfingen sits between two bare krantz topped hills. Here there is friendly chat, and we buy pastries with cream and strawberries. Later we lunch on treacle and vollkornbrot. We cycle on through ranges of hills topped in green. (Like the Natal midlands I think). Still the subtle

Nordlingen: St George's church with housing around it (JT)

washed quality of after-storm light. Then a flat plain and a Roman road to Nordlingen. We cycle in through an arched entrance in its wall. A wagon of hay brushes between the learning houses which are painted in arid pastel colours. The church, golden stone, is a marvel of symmetry in contrast. Out again through a band of houses built against the wall, which is topped by a roofed gallery with slit windows. The tiled gate looks Tibetan to me.

    John:     More pumpernickel and black treacle!

On we go through plains country until around a bend we see the hilltop cluster of Harburg Castle. The tower is lower down amongst the chimneys of a cement factory. A gorgeously medieval sight, with rocks and half-timber and a fantasy white topped lanceolate gable. Then we cycle down into the chasm below Harburg, and rocket down a cobbled street between crazily hanging houses, the castle towering above the side alleys. Glimpse a cart of pastel hay crossing a bridge. We barrel out of the town past a shop full of burnt carcases, an old barn, and – in the afternoon heat – along a rolling road to Donauworth. We pass a swimming pool crowded with bodies, see a disembodied town floating in the valley seemingly hanging from a white turnip domed tower. Reach the echoing, thick-walled hostel. Lie and write up my journal. Supper is two eggs, soup, potato, strawberries. We watch a storm move across the green hills, mist isolating and then obliterating pink roofs, rain filing itself against the double panes, wind banging the grey shutters. Early to bed. Sleep long and sound. A feeling of great comfort.

Steinach: Tulip dome seen across a wheat field (JT)

DAY 41
MONDAY JUNE 15
AUGSBURG / STEINACH / MUNICH

From Donauworth there is the dull agony of the flat, straight Roman Road. Could the Roman soldiers, walking far from home, have enjoyed this? Or would they have felt horribly alone? Augsburg has straggling ragged outskirts. A crossroad is completely dug up. The road diverts between old flats, plastered classical amongst trees. We press on towards "Munchen".

Leon: Why I wonder, did the Bauhaus not feature on our list? Maybe only Dessau was known to us then.

We cycle on the old man-worn, beast-wandered road, trees – now gnarled and old, now flashy and young, lining and shading the tarmac. The country rolls in unfenced fields of wheat. The day is sombre, moisture darkened clouds hang in the sky. Menacing banks of conifers jut out into the fields, darkly enclosing. Before the threatening storm people work in the hay, raking, turning, pausing. Villages fold out of creases like the seams in a turned-out cushion. The horizon is fingered with white spires with turnip domes. There is a cluster of tightly eaved red-tiled houses, the road swinging round in and up into a village passing a Gasthof. There are barns with wide overhang, intricate woodwork, arch-topped wooden doors giving glimpses of farm treasures: sacks, old wheels, axles. Small peasant dwellings with stables and living spaces joined and, at Steinach, we see the turnip dome grow red in a field of wheat.

John: One of my Trip64 pic's shows all of this, it seems. In the 60's and 70's the AJ and the AR architectural magazines always wanted to take cheat shots of newly completed buildings from under branches of a tree, presumably to make it look less new. Amusingly, there was the famous shot of some building with at the top of the shot a hand holding a twig to get the "taken from below a tree" cheat shot. My pic is genuine, but it could have been a cheat!

The shop proclaims "Lebensmittel" – sausages, pastries, sweets and breads. Cycle on down through woods, up through hay being rushed into barns and then we reach the shaggy edge of Munich. Here there is a change: a pulsating city heart has attracted this flotsam, it has purpose. The cobbled road rattles excited. We reach the station. People, more people. Doing things going places. The place buzzes. Women are smartly dressed. On to the hostel, before the rain. A letter from my mum: the joy of reading and relating. We've made it here! München atmosphere! Sleep.

Munich: Richard Strauss fountain (LvS)

DAY 42
TUESDAY JUNE 16
MUNICH-1

The day starts painfully. Puncture, laundromat 'automaat', barber. The barber cuts from the back to the front! We take a tram to the Hofbahnhof, clinging on. Out into streaming people, we make for the Stadtische Galerie and the Paul Klee exhibition we've been aiming to see. Muscles aching our walking is desultory. Cataclysm! A pastry window we cannot pass. In and we have one and an iced coffee – my first ever! The Gallery, an old orange fossil, metal cactus, pots and encrustations. We have hot chocolate in the eating-patio. The atmosphere is free, and our mood is set. There is an exhibition of work by Muncheners, which I find exhilarating, and I am itching to get going myself. We rise through a Kandinsky kaleidoscope; I don't get this. Where is Klee? The wardens here are looking at the pictures. At last, a room of early Klees – those two horrors: the woman in the tree: Virgin in the Tree 1903; and the two bending men, greeting: Two men Meet, Each Believing the Other to be of Higher Rank (1903). But also – oh joy! – a street scene: Strassen Kreuzung (1911), the lines all hurtling to the vortex vanishing point. The subtle blue wash and yellow and orange of Stilleben mit Gietkan (1910). The line and wash in Vorsicht Nord München (1913), pencil first, ink later. Bit of an anti-climax follows in the Blaue Reiter room, yet fascination grows. Helmut Hoffman, Blumen, stamped on. Fauve portraits by Gabriel Munter (1817–1962). Then another room of Klee, fully fledged into what I love. I can hardly contain my excitement! Lote (1925): posts reflected in water? Stern Verbundene (1923): tones of brown to yellow, block figures, black figures, folded tissue effect. In der Einde (1921): a scream suspended, wonky eyed foreshortened lady on parchment, pen and wash. A masterpiece! Who else could use a page of parchment so well? Fraulein von Sport (1938): stick figure black brush, brown background, humour; blue strips top and bottom; it sings! There is no stopping now!.

    Leon:    This enthusiasm for Klee did not last and is certainly not with me now!

On to the two-day whirl of Munich. We have lunch on the patio: coke, vollkornbrot and sardines. Terrific! Then we cut across a windy neoclassical square – Konigsplatz – ask at a bookshop for directions to a stationers – a fab girl directs us – an even better girl at the stationers. We walk back streets and reach a main shopping street. Another cafe: pastry and coffee! To hell with the expense! With cares! With everything! Walk up and down, go into department stores and

Munich: John in the Hofbrauhaus (LvS)

supermarkets deciding what is admirable, what not. We pick out a portable typewriter as exemplary!

It's 5 PM and everyone is shopping. The displays come alive! There are rabbits in the chemist's window! Men are selling foot spray, shouting at the tops of their voices, using all sorts of disgusting props: models of cut open feet, old shoes, a guinea pig and a mysterious bubbling apparatus. A woman explains the merits of a combing technique, using a wig. A man sells a cure-all by flourishing batches of testimonials and reading from them. We swim through the tide of jostling people; the fountain falls silent to the sound of their feet.

We seek out the Hofbräuhaus, expecting an anti-climax after the bustling street. Down alleys, past a bakery selling rough brown bread, hearing the baker above the roar of channelled water, round a corner and there it stands, streaming flags. In through the arches, it is full. Vast benches of people talking, singing, drinking. Some are eating their own packed suppers, after work. Waitresses with three tankards in each hand stumbling between the pillars in their rush to keep up. Others carry trays of radishes, buns with gherkins and ham, pretzels, bread in sticks. There is a group in lederhosen. We sit on a bench and talk to our neighbours, an engineer from Hamburg on one side, two American students on the other. A man in a mustard suit curses us for speaking English, and the engineer says "We are not all like that. Especially those like me who are from the north."

Out into the gasse, blissfully heady, pass through an arch and I am rooted to the spot by the intricate plasterwork on a wall. We pass up the shopping street again, now quiet and the fountain lit. Tram to hostel. Bleary sleep.

(above) Munich: Drinkers in the Hofbrauhaus (JT)
(below) Munich: Dome of Justizpalast (JT)

```
DAY 43
WEDNESDAY JUNE 17
MUNICH-2
```

Start the day going to the Kunsthaus through back streets, the classical buildings weirdly orange in the morning light. Pass the grey bulk of the national theatre, note the side thrust of the triple arched Feldherrnhalle facing medieval into the neo-renaissance street. Before all is the statue and the facade of the Maximilianeum poured red across the limit of the street. I cross through an arch and am in a park, colonnaded. Pop my head back and it is all street! Sandwiched between neoclassical facades is the squeezed baroque front of St Johann Nepomuk, the Asam Church (1733–1746). Amazed by the painted vault melting into sky. At the Kunsthaus there is a Henry Moore reclining woman. Kunst is for the wealthy. Carry on to the university; I'm tired and the street is grandiose.

```
    John:     I believe I spent the morning drawing some of the
              classical buildings before meeting Leon for lunch.
```

**Meet John for a miserable lunch in another brauhaus.**

```
    Leon:     Were we miserable or was it the food? I don't recall.
    John:     This could well have been our second (and last?)
              "temper tantrum" experience, following the first on
              or soon after Day 34. If it was, I think it would
              have been that I wanted a day off culture and a
              static day drinking and drawing. My first drawing in
              Munich I tracked down to possibly Karlsplaz near
              the Hofbrauhaus and the next six maybe inside the
              Hofbrauhaus. I was anxious to improve my pen and ink
              drawing technique using the same subject matter as in
              the pub in Cookham. When back in UK, at some point, I
              did a sketch based on my Hofbrauhaus drawings.
    Leon:     We wander letting the streets take hold, pass
              holidaying couples. Have coffee and soggy pastries in
              a cafe. Carry on exploring the narrow side streets,
              seeing everywhere, up this alley, over those roofs,
              'the twin towers of the Dom'. John takes photos, we
              are laughing and talking and looking. At the hostel
              shower and sleep.
```

(above) Munich: Leaving early in the morning (JT) and Wasserburg: Our bikes watching people, while in the cool arcade we bought things for lunch (LvS)
(below) Wasserburg: Town of stepped gables and a chalky river (JT)

DAY 44
THURSDAY JUNE 18
ALTENMARKT

We leave the city through its edge straggle and enter pleasant rolling countryside, day-dreaming and relaxed. One field rolls on another, conifers green and light, villages pass in pleasant repetition. We buy bread and peppermints from a small store. "Gute Fahrt!" Eat under some conifers. The road lazes up and on. We turn right through trees and left and down and there stand enormous, stepped gables abutting a rushing, gurgling river, and the road hurtles us into the chasm via a hairpin bend. We pop out into a main square of tall, faded-pastel plaster facades, all boxed and shuttered and raised up on the arched flanges of a colonnade, cool and white in the shade. Our eyes are let out at one end, to a small white chapel beyond.

    We lunch on the banks of the chalky river where it cuts its way into a chalk cliff above bushes. We soak in the sun. Round loaf, cheese and peanuts. We return to the coolth of the honeycomb passageways and cycle round to the bridge. Looking back, we see a piling up of dwelling upon dwelling, hanging balconies casting different weights of shadow. We stand-pedal up out of the chasm into countryside that is more interesting than that of the morning: hills, bends, apple trees, light and suspended shade, cool Gasthofs, hanging eaves, tucked-in balconies, wood stacked in triangles against the walls of barns and houses, a sense of the alpine.

    The shirt is clammy on my back, and I discard it and fly, the wind in my armpits, down through fields of haymaking; the hay strung out on fences or on posts in lines. Fieldes edge into woods, woods elbow into fields. Browned women are raking, hammering, laughing. We push up the sticky tarmac of the road, dripping sweat. Enter a Gasthof, pine-panelled, smelling of potato salad and sausages, sweet beer and smoky evenings. A waitress irons fluffy aprons that hide her money pouch, A farm worker hot and seed-itching buys mineral water. The sticky day goes on.

    At Altenmarkt, under the bridge, we can see the stones through the clear, snow-melt water as it gurgles and batters its way down to the sluggish chalk valley. Traunstein has a pleasant town square. The hostel is in a suburban house and the warden is friendly. Helps me fix a puncture. We have soup, bread and then coffee. A noisy friendly group, but talk is difficult. I write up my journal until late.

A village church as Salzburg approaches (JT)

DAY 45
FRIDAY JUNE 19
TRAUNSTEIN TO SALZBURG

We cycle up a narrow, conifer-bound valley; fields twist and are combed neat. The tiled roofs of barns overhang the road. Spend my last German money (50pfg) on sweets. Stopping, looking, rolling, sucking. First glimpse of the mountains, silhouetted blue above morning mist. High-heartedly wish this could go on forever. The mountains are ever closer, their bulk in contrast with the gravity defying byzantine spires of village churches. The mountains now look sunk into the earth, then they rise up, and now seem to give in, and then rise to overhang us with a triumphant pinnacle. Grey rocks line conifer flanks, the road takes us to the border, to customs and an information service. We find Salzburg cluttered between mounds in a valley.

    We cycle to Hugo von Hofmannsthal Straße, to the house of the Couzyns. Dawie is an opera singer (1925–2005, baritone, had his debut at the Albert Hall in 1955 and with the Chamber Opera in Austria) married to my father's cousin Babs Coetzee. They have a daughter Nicky, our age, and a younger son Victor. We are expected, but there is no one home. We carry on to the hostel and check in our bikes. Wander down a narrow street cluttered with little shops. Appetising cooking smells assail us. Mounds of chocolate too. We cross a bridge facing a flat facade topped by the rocky promontory and the Festung (Fortress) Hohensalzburg. Through an arch we enter a fantastic honeycomb of pedestrian shopping alleys, curving left and right, canopied with the metal forest leaves of shops signs. We pass tides of people. Arches lead off into darkness, tunnels lead to courtyards, beer gardens, restaurants, patches of light, the debris of small factories. We emerge into the Residenzplatz, gravel from side to side, an equestrian fountain spouts water in front of the Dom. An arcing colonnade leads to another courtyard, to St Peterskirken. Inside is a big white room ornately plastered. We judge the murals as weak but admire two balconies, one glazed and the other a pulpit, both picked out in white and gold. Walk out into a courtyard, light framed by wrought iron. Enter St Peter's Keller and, sitting in an alcove cut out of the rock of the Festung, drink long cool white wine.

    Tracing our way back to the hostel we enter the damp darkness and looming pillars of the Franziskanerkirche, candles flickering, highlighting dark wooden pews, a baroque altar lit up with more candles. Sitting in Romanesque darkness, we are blanketed in a medieval gloom. Then when

Salzburg: Looking down from the Festung (JT)

we turn, we face light shafted onto the altar, the pillars freed from gravity thrusting up simple and right, space spreading, opening out beyond walls. In an alley shop I buy a Pelikan Pen (black and green). We enter the Wiezl Gallery – Kokoschka on display. I'm not keen, but there is a fine selection of books, a coffee bar and an artists' club. From the hostel we go to Hofmannsthal Strasse, rooibos tea and a big welcome from all. On the way back to the hostel we watch the flickering light of torches as it seems to set the arches in motion.

Salzburg: The horse fountain in Residenzplatz (JT)

DAY 46
SATURDAY JUNE 20
SALZBURG-2

In the morning we transfer our baggage to the Couzyn's house and cycle down to the Dom where there is a market under canvas and bright umbrellas. There are piles of small farm produce: radishes, tomatoes, strawberries, cherries, cheese, meat in stacks, some of it in sacking, eggs in baskets, and bread cut and sold by weight. The bread is mainly rye, but some has a honey-coloured crust and a currant-black centre. Around this are stalls selling rolls, wurst and mustard. There are spring mountain flowers such as we have seen along the roads and in fields while cycling here; picked before mowing, lovely alpine everlastings.

    Up alleys and then steps, through arched hole to the Festung where we sit on a wide top wall and watch the spires of Salzburg. Tucked between valley walls are the river and midget traffic. Further up we come to a long-vaulted passageway with light punching through the thick walls onto the whitewash and gravel floor. People are silhouetted against the light at the far end. In the castle complex we find an inn, a museum, an art school. There are more faceted arches and pillars to one side. We go through to a terrace and now look down onto the spires, seeing also the sprawl of the city up the flattening valley to the mountains, beyond the historic core. There is haymaking directly below us, the sound of a hammer falling on a drying stake reaching us when the stroke is on the up.

    Down through the town and shops, out across the river, through the classical hotel and business sector to the station.

    Only 165 schillings to Venice!

    More exploration of the shopping alleys then lunch with the Couzyns: rice, peas, mince and chives! In the afternoon we all go out in the car – my first drive for a month and a half!

Leon: The car was a Vauxhall Velox, the last model with chromium flutes on the bonnet; possibly a carry-over from Dawie's time in England.

Dawie Couzyn takes us all to swim in lake Fuschl. The route takes us out of the tremendous heat of the valley up into mountain country. We pass people still madly making hay. Nestled in conifers we come upon the blue of the lake. The mountains tower over, some in cones, others leaning away and presenting long, brittle looking krantzes. We drive along a farm road to a sunny cove, strip and float for an hour and a half, looking at the blue sky and the conifer clad mountains, chatting and laughing. Later we walk along the banks of the

Salzburg: The horse fountain in Residenzplatz (JT)

lake through stone pines feeling like characters from Swallows and Amazons. Coffee and rich peasant cake on a Gasthof porch that overhangs the water, rippling away to the far side. Clouds come up, mist appears on the peaks, settles, clings. Haze grows and the air chills. We climb through the woods gathering wood for a promised 'braaivleis' (BBQ). There are shoals of spiky white-starred and blue-trumpeted flowers. Dawie has gone to fetch the car and we walk across a mown field to the road. In a dip we see the blue of the Fuschl below us. The mist turns the mountains into silhouettes, isolating then obliterating, banking against cliff tops and furling over.

    We return through Thalgau, driving on gravel roads through the woods and fields, past farmsteads. Pass a tractor giving a lift to small children on its mudguards. A pine covered white rock cliff towers over a neatly tucked in field. Up and around and hairpin down, far along the valley we see the thick rain front, and we approach it via Thalgau with its Gasthof, eaves and stacks of sheltered wood. Out onto the autobahn, we pass the Mondsee covered in drizzling mist, then the rain streams our windows and in our dark cosiness we glimpse small, neat valleys. Flashes of lightning, streets running with water. Quietly happy, I enjoy the dry South African humour of Dawie. In the evening we cluster around the fire in the garden, drips falling from the trees, a sky chasing across the peaks. Pork chops, thick polenta and grilled potatoes ... In our room I lie in the half light and listen to music being played downstairs, looking at Babs's black and white felt pen drawings on the walls. I worry about my sketches. They are not where my heart is ... I feel suspended, but I am thinking and seeing.

    `Leon:     In that order? See my book DSSD 2020 in which I argue the converse.`

Some of what I've seen in galleries has given me a terrific kick. I want to do something with wood stacks, and movements through arches. Have a slight stomach-ache from eating so much after our pared back travel diet. Beard on or off? Oh, forget it Leon! Sleep soundly.

(above) Salzburg: Various cupolas and the tower on Residenz Palace (JT)
(below) Salzburg: Boring but accurate drawing of houses at rear of the Couzyn's house (JT)

DAY 47
SUNDAY JUNE 21
SALZBURG-3

Sleep late. Breakfast on toasted rolls. Spend the morning quietly reading books – Bosman short stories that also have the dry Afrikaner wit that Dawie has. Chatting and joking he drives us out on the autobahn in the mist to visit the Mondsee. Everything is different in the mist. A woolly sifting of clouds through the banks of pines, sometimes suspending trees in spiky isolation, sometimes rubbing them out. There is only the vague suggestion of the towering bulk of the mountains. A four-turnip spire stands out against the mist in the distance and close up a single spike and tiled ball. At the Mondsee cliffs rise sheer from the lake surface, cloud suggesting an immensity of height. Babs tells us of the cruel count whose moon-shaped territory sank away as a punishment. On the Attersee we see a fisherman standing in his boat black against the brilliant light of the water, pine-stabbed cliffs running in ravines of mist and water. We walk through a dripping wood to a 'klamm' – a rushing mountain stream gouging its way from waterfall to pool, round in and down through the rock. We stand on a wooden bridge, exposed to the rain, the mountains directly above us and look down into the rushing chasm, white with torn rock. Light shines through dripping leaves. Nicky wears my jacket.

    We drive on up a small pass, every patch of usable land is cropped. Down to the river Traun and along to the Traunsee which looks as green and limitless as the sea. The road takes onto the cliff bank and then across the water the cliff rises sheer into the clouds. We stop and gaze into the green chalky water rippling against the rocks where the tunnel was cut, young pines in silhouette on a tongue of land, which becomes the upturned spoon promontory of Traunstein and Traunkirche. We walk past moorings in the neck hearing the lake sizzling in drizzle. Walk up and along to the church, darkly womb-like baroque inside, statues backlit against stained glass, a pulpit comprised of a net of silver fish hauled up by two figures. Strains of Bach in flight come from the organ. In the graveyard I see the lake through a forest of frilly wrought iron crucifixes.

    We drive back down the valley to the Wolfgangsee, the white church of St Wolfgang stabbing across the lake. St Gilgen is a country town church. It has a green roof, a bulb tower, and inside there is a gallery and there are numbers and nameplates on the pews. In the churchyard, through an arch between cypresses, I see the roof three times triangularly punctured by dormers. We descend into Salzburg, the

Salzburg: John's drawing confidence grows in alleyway in town (JT)

Festung hovering above, towers stretching the length of the valley. Spend the evening crowded into the kitchen, joking and laughing somewhat hysterically . . .

Salzburg: Looking down from the Festung onto the cathedral (JT)

DAY 48
MONDAY JUNE 22
SALZBURG-4

I leave my bicycle in the Linzergasse for repairs, walk to the Marktplatz for information about galleries where a friendly girl directs us to the Residenzplatz which I reach through arches and alleys, looking in through openings, watching for attractions. Stumble down one alley and, looking, up find rising white arched balconies. The galleries are all very disappointing, nothing but Kokoschka. I try the Dom. A boring interior and an infuriating notice: "Enter the house of God decently dressed, ladies and gentlemen." I meet John and we have iced coffees in a cafe off the pedestrian street: newspapers in cane holders, tables in cubicles – dark sitting comfort. A headline suggests that Edward Kennedy has died, but it's merely my poor German.

We walk out to a quieter part of the town beyond Mozartplatz. Here renaissance classical buildings have deep entrances leading to the light of inner courtyards. Architraves are picked out in wrought iron curlicues. There are striking glimpses of the castle overhead. And yet all is grey. Up a gasse we see the towering bulb of the Nonnberg, dirty russet with echoing triangular gable blocks, echoed again in the castle.

At the Couzyns I bury myself in a book of Henry Moore shelter sketches, listening to Bach. Back into town for more wandering. It rains. I return depressed, tired of moving on, bored with sketching towns (I don't have an analytical framework to make the drawings interesting), longing for a chance to settle in and do some work. Buy some crayons from Ivo Haas, planning on a change of technique. Admire and photograph the small orange bulb of Michaelskirche on the Residenzplatz. It is bounded massively on three sides. Gains my love for the gap between it and the Residenz. Try drawing that. As I move about, the fountain often fills this gap and there is the constant backdrop of the pine covered mount. Horses and coaches stand against the Dom on the gravel. More views through arches.

```
Leon:      Frames framed became the title for later works that I
           made.
```

I love, also, the way the Kollegienkirche rises brown and bow fronted, two-towered, above the town's non-committal river facade, leading me to expect a triumphal space within the mass of the town. However, there is only a narrow gap and the linked square centres on the Dom.

Sleep off my depression.

Salzburg: Market day (JT)

## DAY 49
## TUESDAY JUNE 23
## SALZBURG-5

Wander through the arch linked inner squares to the festival theatre which is carved into the rock. Look in on the backstage. Back in the neoclassical part of the town, beyond the bottleneck of a gasse, I find a golden stone pavement. I sit in the sun sketching the now mud-red bulb of the Nonnberg, the intricacies of the gasse, the patterns of the castle – grey flanks with black punctured openings and a floating turret. Little girls, coming out from school – all skirts, satchels and knees – watch me and I draw them. People come through the gasse, pause and move between the orange facades on my other side. Pigeons land fan-like and scatter in a thick cloud. The morning is over before I know it. Wander back for lunch crossing the bridge and watching the towers rise out of the town and the castle recede.

    Afternoon. Walk in the suburb at the foot of the Gaisberg, happily and quietly watching the castle which from here is quite whole and medieval. It is slightly misty and there is a faint suggestion of mountains behind. With Nicky and John, I climb a lusciously grassy hillock covered in the starred blue and piped white wildflower. We sit on top watching the sun go down, the castle thrusting up pink, the valley mouth disappearing in haze, the river winding silver through trees to the valley apex. We move round to the other side of the mound and see far to the north rolling green on rolling green spiked with towers, and closer the cropped fields neat against woodland. A pale orange church in its graveyard, capped by a single rust bulb with dates on it: 17XX–1883, 1885–1934. Directly below us people are playing ball. We walk down and round, chatting and blowing noises on grass reeds, joking. At the church in a little wrought iron enclosed shrine, we see an altar depicting purgatory. There are cardboard flames, and in small, redlined boxes piled up the walls, skulls. Carefully tagged and dated in baroque script. Gruesome. Back up the hill on wooden steps to a wooden shack where we reach the level of the bell tower just as the bells start to ring throughout the valley and ours swing. We see the light shell and then the dark mouth, back and forth for some minutes. We lean on a rail fascinated. It stops but the bell still swings, the wooden arm creaking this way and that in the sun-touched calm.

    The sun is out for the last time and we walk back to find Dawie making boerewors in the kitchen. Braaivleis follows. All of us on the grass, lying on red Basuto blankets, watching

Salzburg: The Festung (LvS)

flames leap and then ripple through the coals, wet grass and wood smoke close me in under the high cloud sky. The sausage and polenta is very good. Chocolate by Suchard – the bitter is good, the milk is too sweet.

Salzburg: View (above) of the Festung and (below) of an alley (LvS)

DAY 50
WEDNESDAY JUNE 24
SALZBURG-6

Morning in the town, Afternoon on the grass hill, the sun out and baking as we bask eating bitter chocolate and watching the castle proud on its ridge. Light shines from behind the tree slab of a closer hut, skittering on the multifaceted blocks of the industrial buildings down the valley. Faded mountains rise up behind the castle, the river flashing up the valley, and my crumpled chocolate paper is a valley in itself. Spikes of trees rise up when I lay on my back. A lovely lazy afternoon. Raw steak for supper – had avoided this in Holland. I like it! When dark we go back on the hill. There is a soft glow on the walls of the street and the castle, floodlit, has become flattened cardboard. There are neon flashes from behind Kapusinerberg, remote and clockwork. A cool breeze through the grass, a hedgehog snorts.

John: I remember to this day the raw steak in Salzburg. I had never eaten such a steak before and none that I have had since have come anywhere near the "Salzburg steak". I watched Leon cook it and couldn't believe it when he handed me our supper with less than a minute on either side – it was out of this world!

Salzburg: A shopping street near the Festung (JT)

DAY 51
THURSDAY JUNE 25
SALZBURG-7

After soaking in the bath, walk past the old town on the riverbank, the towers and domes floating above bankside houses criss-crossing against the grey green HohenSalzburg. Visit exhibitions in the Mirabell Casino, but nothing holds my attention. Up the Linsergasse through an arch to the stations of the cross, groups of painted statues lined up the Kapuzingerberg, saying "how do you do?" to rather pathetic looking saints. Back down through the cut and thrust of roofs along the gasse.

John's money has come!

In the evening we drive up the Gaisberg with Babs and Dawie, past the overhanging eaves and wood stacks, combed and striped fields edged into forest. The sun sinks behind the moving uprights of crossing tree trunks. The valley is hung in a sun pink mist, the blue edge of the Alps rising in cloud above closer, sun stained and glossy fir trunks. The sun setting across the distant Bavarian flatlands, slicing behind clouds, and on the summit, we find the chipped and wood-flaked bricks of a ruin, the ashes of an equinox fire. Down passing rally practicing cars.

Sleep early and long – tomorrow we go to Venice. It is time to leave, but the Couzyns made us a home here and I will miss them.

John: I shared Leon's pleasure of staying with his relatives in Salzburg. After 51 days on the road for Leon, only ½ that for me, a week of being in one place with a delightfully welcoming and interesting family doing normal things like cooking, enjoying family life, a bit of home working (lots of dictation was going on related to a boy's Mozart choir) was just what was needed before our attack on Italy. It also gave my brain the chance to really think about improving my pen and ink drawing skills and take in properly what help Leon was giving me. By the time I did the last of my Salzburg sketches, I felt I was actually getting somewhere. Thank you so much the Couzyns!

Leon: Except for a cursory rendezvous in Florence described later, I never saw any of them again. Largely because Babs, my father's blood relative, died soon after these meetings, falling from an express train in Spain. Worse befell the rest of the family when they returned to South Africa.

DAY 52
FRIDAY JUNE 26
TO VENICE

At Hugo von Hofmannsthal Strasse we spend the morning preparing and having a farewell tea. The train leaves at 2PM. It pulls out of Salzburg rising up the valley and we see again the deep eaves, wood piles, green fields, haymaking, fenced and staked drying hay. The train stops at all stations. In the station yards timber is stacked, varying diameters and lengths, the round ends facing us, shadows between. There are boxes of chippings, some triangular, some sections of a cylinder. Stacks of twigs. Water streams out grey rocks in streaks. Form fitting hill farms sweep by. A man in the carriage is doing a crossword. I itch to draw his bulbous sculptural form, baggy eyes, balding head. We pass through tunnels with the rise and fall of their safety lines becoming hypnotic. Flashes of light burst in from avalanche refuges. We read The Times, and lookout at the rocky heights.

    Tunnel through to Hofgastein, the train now high above the valley to Bad Gastein, hotels on the hill. Flashes of mountain streams, fields climb up with us, small hay huts dotted about, bare tops of mountains are smooth and bald. Think of a walking holiday here. The train clatters high above a flat valley, winding roads, winding cars, villages in map format, light haze. A white turnip towered church is isolated in confers above us. We reach a widening valley and at Villach, commuters board. The train is heading with growing commitment towards Treviso and Italy! The countryside growing wilder in the afternoon light. At Treviso the train stops for border checks. Customs officials come on board. I stand alone outside in a rushing wind. Even the buildings look wilder. Terracotta and faded orange. Nattily uniformed police in blue and navy-blue chatter away. Men sell cold pasta and ice cream. John's beard provokes chin stroking: "Christo! Christo! Capito?" Rippling chatter in Italian comes from the next compartment. The train pulls out in the evening light. I watch wild and jagged mountain peaks, trees are wilder, fields are less neat. Still Alpine. There are tin roofs! Some shiny and new, some rusting. There is another roofing material, blue-black and looking like bundled twigs. Is it slate? More and more stone. Between stations I try to sleep on the bench and do. Excitement grows in me as does anticipation. See a floodlit church, pillared and canopied, triangle and circle segment capped windows, coloured plasterwork, shaggy trees, the smell of dust! At stations, the bubbling sound of talking, the calls of hawkers.

    Just before we reach Venice, we are woken by two Italians coming into the compartment. We arrive after midnight.

Venice to Rome

TIMELINE PART 3 - ITALY

| Day 53 | Saturday - Venice - from midnight - 1 | YH Venice S. Giacomo |
|---|---|---|
| Day 54 | Venice - 2, Lido et al | YH Venice S. Giacomo |
| Day 55 | Venice - 3 | YH Venice S. Giacomo |
| Day 56 | Venice - 4 | YH Venice S. Giacomo |
| Day 57 | Venice - 5 | YH Venice S. Giacomo |
| Day 58 | Venice - 6 | YH Venice S. Giacomo |
| Day 59 | To Padua and Vicenza | Take SR11 W from Venice to Padua, ghosting a canal. 2h23. Continue on SR11 to Vicenza 1h58. Sleep out near V. Rotondo |
| Day 60 | Vicenza / Po valley | SW then S, on SS434 to Baruchella. Then E to Bagnolo di Po. 4h24. Sleep out under vine, woken by rain |
| Day 61 | Vino Dolci at Runzi / Ferrara / Argenta / Ravenna / | SP12 via Ferrara to Argenta. 3h8. Shelter 2h. SP 16 to Ravenna. 2h4. Locanda Dei Melarancio, via Mentana. |
| Day 62 | Ravenna | Locanda Dei Melarancio |
| Day 63 | Ravenna to Porta di Ki | SP34 SW along canal, then S to Forli. 1h41. SS67 to Castrocaro. 40m. SS67 to San Benedtto in Alpe. Acquacheta Valtancoli ristorante. 2h9. Press on a few kilometres. Sleep out on roadside. |
| Day 64 | Down to Florence | SS67 to Dicomano. Continue along SS67 via San Francesco to Florence. 3h29. YH Florence |
| Day 65 | Florence - 1 | YH Florence |
| Day 66 | Florence - 2 | YH Florence<br>"Vittore! I don't want to go to Venezia!" |

(left) YHA badge on John's rucksack
(right) John's sheath knife

| | | |
|---|---|---|
| Day 67 | Florence - 3 | Pensione Serena 'a room of our own for a few days!' 'Innerspring mattresses!' |
| Day 68 | Florence - 4 | Pensione Serena |
| Day 69 | Florence - 5 | Pensione Serena |
| Day 70 | Florence - 6 | Pensione Serena, 'meal of bread and water to make up for lunch' |
| Day 71 | To Pisa / Livorno / Coast | SS67 westwards to Pisa. 4h47. E80 W and then S along the coast to Livorno. 1h28. SSE on SS1 to Tombolo Beach. 2h56. Sleep on beach under pines |
| Day 72 | Via Aurelia | E80 to Civitavecchia. 10h2. Sleep on another beach. Cycle through the night SW to Rome on SS1. 3h44. |
| Day 73 | Civitavecchia / Rome (Friday July 18) | Albergo del Sol |
| Day 74 | Rome and end of day-by-day journal entries. | |
| Day 81 (?) | Train to Lausanne? (Saturday July 25) | Overnight on train: about 9h. |
| Day 82? | Lausanne international exposition | Overnight train to Paris. About 6h. |
| Day 83? | Paris to Boat train to London, Bourne End; | About 12 h. Bourne End, pushing the bike down drive, father sees me and says: "never mind, we will soon feed you up!" |

TIMELINE PART 3

```
DAY 53
SATURDAY JUNE 27
VENICE-1
```

We arrive after midnight.
The train runs along a link to the city

```
John:     The "link" was/is in fact a long rail and road manmade
          link across the Laguna Veneta from Mestre to Venice
          and the Statione di Venezia Santa Lucia. The Golfo
          Venezia is beyond Venice, the Adriatic Sea beyond that
          and finally the Mediterranean.
```

I see the lights of ships, a full moon shining orange, in the water rippling. Cars are tearing along the strip

Just look. Too tired to wonder about what to expect, not able to think of beginning or ending, or of the passing of time. Bleary eyed we get out of the train, collect our bikes, have a coke. We exit the station feeling nowhere but in a dream. We walk our bikes to a car park and leave them in the care of the friendly attendant. "Arrivederci!" We sit on the edge of the canal, water lapping at white marble steps, cool and inviting. Streetlights and the moon give light. Buildings suggest themselves and suddenly it strikes me: we are here and it's unbelievably unreal. Faded grey chalky volumes of cylindrical columns, the half cylinder apse, a green dome above. We walk along and then up white steps, the bag straps digging into our shoulders, dully aching. I am above and outside, an observer.

```
John:     I remember vividly our getting off the train from
          Salzburg on our arrival in Venice despite having been
          there a year or two before. Why, I cannot remember
          - there were so many feelings I had at the time. Was
          it how different it was compared with north of the
          Alps, the pride of actually reaching Italy from the
          UK by push bike (except the bit over the Alps of
          course), the relief of leaving after about 12 hours
          on rigid timber seating on the train, the pleasure of
          dumping off our bikes with a cheerful (and hopefully
          trustworthy) man in an office with windows (don't
          know why I remember the windows), the excitement
          that we were about to begin our slow moving journey
          down the leg of Italy or thinking about starting
          studying architecture in the autumn. I was spoilt for
          choice. This was followed by a long walk in the early
          hours of the morning along narrow pathways between
          comparatively tall buildings and over endless canals
          arriving at St. Marks Square at dawn on the opposite
          side of the island. I could have burst with pleasure.
```

Through dark and narrow gaps between buildings, lit by naked bulbs. Up over canal-leaping bridges, faced within a blank

(above) Venice: St Mark's at dawn after early hours walk across Venice from the railway station on our arrival from Salzburg (JT)
(below) Venice: St Mark's western façade (JT)

wall, gap left, gap right. Mewling scattering cats, banging shutters, rippling plaster, moon shadows on terracotta. The fantastic completeness of the suggested form of a church projecting its vault ends into an internal square, deserted. Into a funnel, under a wrought iron balcony covered in creeping plants, metal shutters punctuated with slits covering shop windows. We, suspended, up, over, pause, on in... We seem to be wandering through endless three-dimensional posters. There is a minute Banca di Roma. Red signs point to 'Per Rialto' and 'S. Marco', black ones name the area 'Galle Divolvo'. Gondolas lap at foot level in water between houses. Slap, slap. Glistening ripples, marble white steps. All compete for reality as we walk with heavy eyelids and aching shoulders.

More steps, moon-white under rippling water, the water slapping at posts and at banks and the black shapes of tethered gondolas. A bridge stands out, white. A house is orange in the moonlight. Punctured gothic arch holes are rimmed in marble. More chalked columns, a reddish one to the right. Chairs on paving. People talk and footsteps echo. A baby cries behind shutters. Every nuance of volume accentuated and exploited by the soft light. Sights up narrow alleyways. Stone paving flat from edge to edge clearly expresses relationships of building to building. A bus boat loading and discharging passengers. Conversations. A young man in a smart lightweight suit tests the engine of a boat taxi, throttling and re-throttling, the sound reverberating in multiple echoes. Bridges rise up away to the right. Reflections. The Grand Canal!

Up steps we step through an archway into a colonnade: San Marco opens out to the crazy domes of the Basilica, the brick tower. Chairs, sleeping pigeons. We plod across the hard surface, not there, yet seeing. Round a corner and face the Palazzo Ducale (Doge's Palace). Two pillars on the water's edge bring our wandering to a halt. We sit at their base facing stone steps, rough posts, gondolas black and pointed slap in the wash. Beyond is the faint suggestion of S Giorgio Maggiore. We sit at the foot of a pillar looking up at a lion's tail. The sky is blue, very blue. Stars visible as if painted there like a stage set. Gondoliers arrive jesting, fishing for crabs, sitting in chairs. A prostitute in a black pullover comes over to us: "Hello Inglish!" We chat amiably. A group of boys out all night pass by, their laughter echoing. Couples in suits and cotton print dresses head home, footsteps echoing. All is set for a theatrical climax, but the dawn comes slowly adding dimension to S Giorgio and S Salute, fraction by fraction. Light lifts out the sides of the tower, fills out the dome, the volumes swelling into pink and white.

Venice: Santa Maria della Salute seen across the Grand Canal (JT)

John: The second big memory of my first day in Venice was arriving in St Marks Square at dawn. The light was astonishing, due to it being by the sea as well as the time of day. A few other luggage-laden people were there, I hope with the same song in their hearts. Two or three attractive, and unladen, young women joined in and one began to speak to me in pidgin English. I was rather flattered until it was pointed out to me that she was a prostitute – not interested in me just whether I had a few lire she could get rid of for me! The sideways knock I received on arrival in Cologne caused by the dramatic juxtaposition of the towering cathedral against the horizontal rail bridge was repeated, but functionally reversed, by the horizontality of the much modelled and decorated cathedral and the verticality and plainness of its adjacent brick bell tower. The dawn turned into day as we looked out across the water to San Georgio Maggiore to the left and Santa Maria della Salute to the right.

"Good morning Inglish" A touch on the knee and she rushes along to an early American: "Yeah, I know. You haven't had a fuck all night. Okay." They disappear. My bum now numb on the pillar base, but the drama of emerging form grows faster. The Doge's Palace columns and set back floor become a pink brick mass. We rise and walk and look as people begin to move about. It is 4.30 AM. The sun begins to warm our shoulders. At last, there is a vaporetto – direction S. Giacomo – across to the hostel in an old warehouse on Giudecca. We check in and sit on the edge of the water looking back to the soaring tower, the bubble domes, the floating facade and the massed risings and ripplings of the gondolas. Venice!

The palace facades become recognisable. We watch them float. One, rough red and classical front, I know well from the AJ (Architect's Journal). To the right the dome of San Salute is slightly off centre. Long to see it forever thus in the azure blue of the morning lull before the subtleties melt away in full light of day.

We take a vaporetto to the Lido, its reverberating engine noise numbing us into a different kind of reverie. Venetians going swimming cram the decks. Vivid colours, drawn black hair, golden brown skins, pink lipstick, long limbs. Men in smart uniforms, blue on blue. Old woman smiling, children playing pat-a-cake, pat-a-cake. Sun pours down as the pink and white encrustations of the facades of Venice recede behind us in a wake of cool green. At stops people move on and off, the engine roaring as the vaporetto hugs the mooring posts. At the Lido there are cool bars under trees. We move along in the hanging heat to a communal bathing beach,

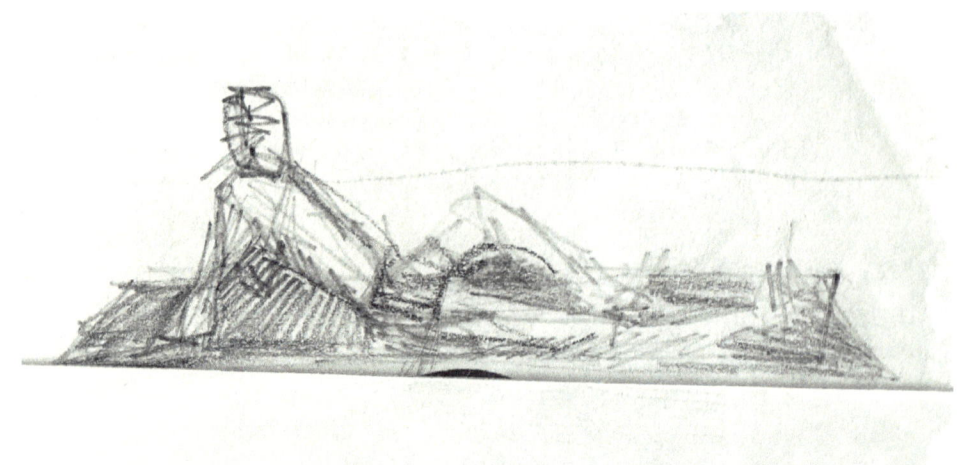

(above) Venice: John at the Lido (LvS)
(below) Venice: A niche in the western facade of St Mark's (JT)

threading our way through the rapid chatter of flouncing mums and scattering children, all waving their arms. John and I swim and play about in shallow warm water – a shock to find that at body temperature it seems not to wet you! We swim and then lie on the beach and sleep in the sun. Feel happy and at home. Our first view of Venice is never to be forgotten. Will my words fail? If so, all fails. Later we swim again and then head back to the hostel where I have my first Italian gelati – marvelling at the distinctive flavours: chocolate, caffe, panne, tortoni, cream . . .

> John: The third and last big memory of my first day in Venice was experiencing the incredible location of the youth hostel and the pleasures inside. The space in front of the hostel was paved with ancient stone slabs out from the face of the building to the water's edge and would have been the unloading and re-loading area for the grain warehouse now converted into the hostel. From this space there was an open 180° view of the main island to the north and many of the buildings on it across the water of what would have been the old port. The conversion from warehouse to hostel was basic, robust and just right. The floor-to-floor heights were big as one would expect in a warehouse and all the timber floor and roof beams were exposed. This accommodated the use of three storey bunk sets, so you got to know your neighbours quite quickly. The tall windows allowed the views across the water to be maintained even when on the top bunk. The Asian lavatories and the showers were also exciting since, until you were an old hand, you wouldn't spot the difference between the two until you had flushed the lavatory after using it and received a shower instead. All of this could be assimilated by drinking the Coca Cola downstairs which seemed to contain a much higher level of caffeine than one was used to in the UK.

We spend the afternoon sitting in San Marco on the steps of the Basilica, of the arcade, absorbing. People, pigeons, the thrusting tower, the pierced facade of the Doge's Palace, the rising columns, the sitting pink brick mass, the setback second floor under that mass, the assemblage of window levels and monuments in cool white plaster and busy carvings. To my surprise the Basilica – at first brash and messy – grows on me, the domes first – floating in juxtaposition to the brick tower. Then the make-up: the walls of collaged marble, pillars of different materials, the setback mosaic murals, the capitols of the pillars, unattached and standing in free space.

Back on Giudecca sit in the evening sun, feet over the marble canal edge and the transparent lapping water. A cafe

Venice: View from the functionally deceptive sanitary facilities in the youth hostel (JT)

spreads its awnings. At the cafe, 'Mama' shouts commands, her sons pull and heave at a white ice cream machine, then bring out pot plants and a neon sign. The sign is lit, a daughter is ready to serve while 'Pappa' supervises... I watch in deep peace as the sun goes down and Venice slips back into subdued light, more red than this morning, now a mysterious and unreal floating strip. Lights go on in the twilight. People are massing here; tanned bodies, rich primary colour clothing, chatting, laughing, greeting each other, friendly and warm. Feel remote. Striking how friendly people are here, comradely. When a son walks into a plate glass window his father roars with laughter, picks the boy up and kisses him and everyone nearby commiserates with the boy, passing the story down the street. Open, unguarded, not defensive. So un-English. To bed under the thick beams of the steep-gabled warehouse. The Beatles boom out on the quayside, which sends a wave of homesickness over me. With effort, before sleeping, I remember to get into my sleeve sheet (a feet-binding ritual at every hostel!) What a marvellous day!

(above) Venice: Part of St Mark's from the courtyard of the Doge's Palace (JT)
(below) Venice: Ca' d'Oro across the Grand Canal (JT)

DAY 54
SUNDAY JUNE 28
VENICE-2

In the morning we go to the station to get a map, the city in morning mood: washed and waiting. Map in hand we repeat the walk of our arrival night. Now the textures stand out: rough bangled tiles, rippling plaster, decayed brick. We recognise the views up alleys and the glimpses of green water slapping at mossy steps. Now clothes are hung out to dry overhead, but the twisting is the same and the leaning circle bridges and views opening and closing are the same. Now there are awnings, chairs, coffee bars, gelati stalls. The volume of S Giacomo dell 'Orio presses to its full extent, gains a stacked roof and a small, ribbed tower. Inside the volume is etched in by ribbing and a painted dome floats above dark paintings. The altar is a simple table, there is a little organ music. A red curtain covers the entrance, wafting as people come in, light candles and leave in a flash of light. Out into a small piazza bounded by a small canal. In daylight the trees are more yellow than green, small-leafed against rich terracotta facades. Shop windows reveal smart clothes or 'Pane' – all white, and wine and cheese. There are shoemakers and small artisanal workshops emit purple light. Arches overhead buttress leaning buildings, pigeons sit on them. At the Grand Canal, so eerily silent last night, vaporetto engines now reverberate. Shops are closed on Sunday, but the bars are open. We sit on steps below a huge wooden door near the Rialto bridge and watch the Sunday parade strolling through trattoria-lined alleyways, dogs with muzzles wander quite freely, there are emaciated cats. Reach again the buzzing Grand Canal with serried barber poles and brick and marble palace facades echoing the motifs of the Doge's Palace, each a picture independently composed. Ca' D'Oro is the standout. Entrances are caves with steps down to the water and lapping slope-backed launches and water taxi boats.

    We cross the Grand canal on a bridge and find our way to the Bridge of Sighs under which gondolas pass, gondoliers in straw hats, blue striped shirts, the narrow water green, the marble so white. We sit drawing in the inner courtyard of the Doge's Palace, picking out Italian trippers peering into the wells. Later we draw the domes of the Basilica, trying to capture the way in which their intersections suggest space. Then the fantasy facade. We watch mums strolling with their sons in military uniform, family parties, kids playing hide and seek between the pillars, chattering picnickers. There are many English tourists, boiled skin colour, gaudy clothes, but all

Venice: Bridge of Sighs (JT)

– good on them – having fun. Lovely girls, groups led by guides. It pours with rain and we join everyone else in walking around in the colonnade. The rain passes, and we cross over the steaming pavers to the columns of San Marco (topped by a lion 'the symbol of St Mark the Evangelist, patron of the city') and of San Todaro (topped by 'a statue of St Todaro, the Byzantine St. Theodore of Amasea, the city's first protector'.) Feel the rising steam on my bare legs. We pass Harry's Bar...

```
Leon:      'legendary 1930s bar famous for its Bellini cocktails'
           - Wikipedia, into which I first went as commissioner
           for the Australian architecture pavilion at the
           Architecture Biennale of 2000. Years later I stayed at
           the Hotel Monaco & Grand Canal, unimaginable luxury -
           both bar and hotel - in 1964.
```

... and we board a vaporetto nearby. In the bright and washed light after rain, we chug across to S. Giorgio Maggiore and on to the hostel on Giudecca (now the Generator Hostel). Watch again as Venice goes dim in the evening light, people again clustering around the cafe, some boys swimming. At the hostel pop songs are playing on the jukebox. Bleary eyed and contented, fall asleep.

Venice: St Mark's (JT)

DAY 55
MONDAY JUNE 29
VENICE-3

Straight to San Marco after breakfast. Draw on the bridge over the canal to the Bridge of Sighs. Then wander in Calles parallel to the Grand Canal glimpsing its busy traffic and bright sunlight. See, through a doorway and a poster covered vault, a terracotta walled courtyard with deep set doors, shuttered windows, a marble well, a rising staircase in wood and pink plaster. In the Campo S. Polo, wide and bare, heat pours up from the stone pavers. It's theatre; I expect a curtain to fall and for actors to emerge at any moment and – applauded – to move on. The Scuolo Grande di San Rocco art museum is strikingly red and rough tiled. Closed today. The redness of most facades is suddenly interrupted by the grey and white chalky lines of a symmetrical classical front. Then again there are views down the tall facets of alleys ending in marble edged steps into cool water. More bridges. Boats carrying cokes and television sets. We draw again in the courtyard of the Doge's Palace. People are resting their tired feet on this feast day of Peter and Paul. Shopping over, bags slumped, balconies piled with bodies sleeping off the heat and lethargy.

    I wander again. Come to the Fish Market on the Grand Canal beyond the Rialto, crustaceans seen in the dark through graceful arches carrying the fabric of small brown brick above. Lovely dark haired, bronze limbed girls wearing electric blue sheaths and pink lipstick surge down the Rialto bridge towards me. Back into the maze and the myriads of pedestrians, the sound of footfalls broken only by the throb of a passing boat. At San Marco, the stage waits. I pause between the twin columns eating a nut bar bought from a small girl and look out across the gondolas to the compact geometry of San Giorgio. Vaporetto to the hostel, shower, sleep.

John in Venice (LvS)

DAY 56
TUESDAY JUNE 30
VENICE-4

Straight to San Marco again. Walk through a new district up along the Grand canal past the Palazzo Cavalli crossing the Ponte dell 'Accademia to the Gallerie Accademia, which is alongside the union jack flying British Consulate, Rah! Rah! In the gallery enjoy the work of Lorenzo Veneziano (1356–1372): two standing figures, S. Marco and S. Picho, placed in their own rectangles, are picked out against gold leaf. In a work by Jacobello del Fiore (1400–1439) I search for a pattern in the foliage. Overall pattern seems also to be the concern of Nicolo de Pietro (1394–1430). These are all altar works with the frames removed, giving rise to probably unintended contrasts with unpainted wood. There are rough edges to the painted surfaces and the occasional doodle. Nicolo floats perspectival flats without a shared vanishing point. A marvellous ceiling above and then the perspective in Madonna e Santi (1505) by Giovanni Bellini (1430–1516) makes me look down. Tintoretto's cartoon-like black and bold strokes depicting bodies shooting in all directions impress the most. La Tempesta (1506–8) by Giorgione (1478–1510) is here! But the impact is spoiled by over familiarity with reproductions. There is a cool polished room with a built-in perspective using fitted paintings and tapered panelling.

    Walk down the pleasantly leafy Rio Terra Foscarini. The bells of S. Agnese hang silhouetted against the sky. Children play ball in a square, chattering noisily. Reach the Canal Della Giudecca, wet and light, windy. Keep walking along the canal, over bridges, glimpsing other canals leading away between brick and tile facades, a few moored boats. The pavement is rough stone edged in marble, a brick balustrade, eaten away at low level, is topped in marble. Green water, speckled chalk grey columns. Then across the Grand Canal the domes of the Basilica appear. Reach the Lanterna Della Dogana where the Giudecca meets the Grand and turn back towards the Dome of S. Salute

    Leon:    on which my first research assistant, Andrew Hopkins, later did his Courtauld PhD. His research is referred to again later.

The portico sits above white steps that rise out of the water and seem to press the facade upwards. Inside there is a domed volume ringed by a colonnade, red light and candle haze. Take a vaporetto to Palazzo Cavlli-Franchetti and cross over the Ponte dell' Academia again.

    Wander through plaster peeling alleys, hanging wisteria blossom, stalls of peaches, bread shops until we reach the

Venice: In and around St Mark's, St Mark's Square and the courtyard of the Doge's Palace (JT)

Campo San Rocco, chalky grey facade stuck onto folding red-orange plaster topped in rustic red tiles. The flash of a red door-hanging, a small semi-circle bridge, gelati stalls with pans of rich colour, coffee shops, playing children. Walk on. Laze chatting on a small bridge behind the Ca Pesaro, soaking in the sun. Vaporetto to San Marco, enter the Basilica wearing jeans and backpacks, feeling uncomfortable. The domes inside are lathered in a smooth pastry crust of golden mosaic, suggesting a carved-out monolith. The floor is a mosaic of marble, there are lumpy slabs of pulpits on granite columns. Women wander about, shawls tucked around their shoulders. A man hisses, selling tickets to the altar. We sit, and slowly recognise the mosaic subjects: the tree of knowledge, the apostles, the stages of the cross. Statues look down, rather dubiously, I think. Wood panelled confessionals, a man shaking an alms box, much adjusting of scarves. Late sun streams in, our necks crick. Back to the hostel and sleep.

John: The more we padded around Venice the more I thought what a very extraordinary place it was, in 1964 that is. The roads you would have expected in any other major centre were replaced by canals and bits of the Laguna Veneta, buildings housing people were not very high due to the cost and practicality of building in water. Attempts to increase the plan area had not been achieved for the same reasons, although easy sea access was there via the Mediterranean, the Adriatic Sea and the Gulf of Venice. One could not actually moor anything very large at the shore, but people wanted to explore Venice. So, you had a town shackled to its medieval form bravely trying to welcome in the 20th century expectations for trade, tourism, culture, etc., and it was doing surprisingly very well to cope.

Venice: Small canal in a slum area (JT)

```
DAY 57
WEDNESDAY JULY 01
VENICE-5
```

On Wednesday we cross the Grand Canal and walk through shopping streets to Calle Loredan on the northern edge of Venice. Sit in early sun under yellow leafed trees, observing the roof geometries, passing people, deliveries by boats. Wander back south towards the Grand Canal. There are these metal trolleys with wheels arranged for riding up steps. Smartly dressed students walk past, each carrying one big book under arms. Smell of bread. Small art materials shops. Small canals, rising bridges, the flash and glow of glass blowing. The Grand Canal is bustling with traffic and spiked with painted poles and jostling palace facades as we Vap back to San Marco, noting the gate to the Guggenheim on the right. At San Marco we ask a policeman in a smart white uniform, solar topi and sword, the way to the Biennale. Bit of a tussle. It is everywhere! We feel like tourists, well we are tourists but now it feels as if the city is a tourist trap. Everything depends on money from tourists. The stalls, photographers who accost us at every turn, the painters doing instant portraits and instant landscapes – even the pigeons!

    We walk along the Grand Canal front towards the Giardini. Divert up an alley of decaying houses and find ourselves at the chalky classical facade of S. Giorgio dei Greci. Tremendous Byzantine interior. Floor in polished cream, red and orange marble squares. The walls are lined with a double row of flip up seats in dark irregular woodwork. Moulded frames around pictures of Madonna and Child, of Saints. Smell of incense. Silver relief portraits. Plaques to the dead. Lectern with ornate inlay supported by twisting candlestick columns. A gallery above the entrance. Then we pass through the Greek Institute to the Museum of Byzantium in which we note the works of the Cretan School: black outlined paintings of S. Giorgio and La Vergine Occulta; a beaten relief in silver with gaps for painted faces, an angel with beaten silver feathers; a papyrus from Ravenna (AC 533); gifts seeking the protection of Archbishops: Emanuel Zanas XVII in particular. Moulded bodies. A Madonna della Passione (XVII) has brown moulding and a very large hand.

    We walk down the canal-side promenade rising over arched bridges and passing arid pastel-coloured clothes hung out to dry. Then we reach the Giardini Publice and the main pavilions of 32nd Biennale di Venice. We see Jose Caballero in the Spanish pavilion; the whimsical punning of Vic Gentils and machine sculptures by Pol Bury in the Belgian. A bulbous

Venice: Sketches of St Mark's square (LvS)

metal sculpture by Arpel in the Dutch. The general exhibition impresses us more: Passmore, Caprogressi, Tapies, Calder, Cezar, Giacometti; some Vasarely style hangings, the blown-up folded paper of a Cagli; the white impressing on white paper of some Savellis in a collaboration with American poets; a wild profusion of platforms in bronze by Cavaliere. Mari is represented by a trompe l'oeil gate and Gruppe Enne Padova have a plethora of mechanised moving illusions.

The other pavilions – Argentina, Bulgaria, Peru, South Africa, Hungary, Israel, Brazil, UAR, Austria, Rumania, Greece, Scandinavia, Switzerland, Venezuela, USSR, Japan, Czechoslovakia, France, Canada, Germany and Italy pass in a blur except for a Rauschenberg jockey in the nude, shades of Duchamp's 'descending a staircase' in the USA pavilion. Johns is here and Nolan and Louis, but all as previously seen in London.

```
Leon:      Wikipedia states: Rauschenberg's selection for the
           1964 Golden Lion marked the United States' ascendancy
           over European artistic dominance, and the entrance
           of pop art into canon. American aggrandisement, even
           the term POP emerged in the UK in Richard Hamilton's
           famous 'This is Tomorrow" collage (exhibited in this
           exhibition at the Whitechapel Gallery, London in
           1956.)
```

In the Great Britain pavilion, there are Hilton's powerful paint masses around figures that seem to have been infilled later; a Tilson Pop picture also previously seen at the Whitechapel in London. A work made of torn paper strips pasted together by Irwin. Maquettes of a Meadows sculpture. At the Biennale book stall there are books about anything except what is in the exhibition!

We return to San Marco up the quayside, bright in the evening sun. At the hostel we have a supper of bread, eggs and carrots and our first Italian wine, which we like. Get quite merry.

Venice: View from the Rialto Bridge (JT)

DAY 58
THURSDAY JULY 02
VENICE-6

To the USA annexe exhibition in a palazzo on the Grand Canal where we see works by Oldenburg – giant typewriter, toaster and telephone made of kapok filled vinyl, cloth and plexiglass; Stella's stripes of colour on raw canvas; Dine's bathroom objects; more Rauschenberg repetitions, symbols and heavily worked surfaces; figure prints by Johns; automobile parts sculptures by Chamberlain. Clearly so engrossed here that a curator gave me a guide ... Itching to get going myself.

> Leon: A note in the journal refers me to an annotated catalogue for this pavilion, which catalogue is now lost.

From here find ourselves amongst glassblowers again and watch the making of candy vases from rods rolled into hollow globules of soft glass. A horse is pinched into recognisable form in under 60 seconds! Walk around the Salute point and spend the afternoon wandering and photographing Ca' d'Oro and the narrow-bridged canals, S. Giacomo dell'Orio and then wide-open paved areas baking in the sun. Campo S. Polo, the roof huddle of the busy Rialto bridge.

> Leon: none of my photos have survived.

Sit under the columns at San Marco. Girls crowd around to be photographed. Lovely soft arms! At the hostel we sup on rolls, eggs, chocolate flake ice cream and wine taking in our last view of Venice glowing softly over the water. Gloat over my trophy from the USA annexe with its gorgeous reproduction of one of Rauschenberg's works. This yank also 'looks'! Early to bed, because we leave in the morning.

(above) Vicenza: Piazza dei Signori with Palladio's Basilica Palladiana to left (JT)
(below) Vicenza: Palladio's Villa Capra "La Rotonda" - posh place to sleep (JT)

DAY 59
FRIDAY JULY 03
TO PADUA AND VICENZA

John: As we left Venice to head south to "normal" towns and cities, I thought more of its struggle to welcome in the 20th century. Little did I know what was going to happen to Venice over the years since 1964. Massive constructions to try to stop it sinking into the sea, continued and worsening flooding, increases in visitor numbers and, worst of all in my opinion, the arrival of the massive multistorey cruise ships that have been invented in recent years, although these have recently been banned. What will happened to this beautiful place?

Collect our bikes from the station and set off. Excited to be back in the 20th Century! I am not like Ruskin. Do not want to live as a hermit amidst the stones of Venice! The road to Padua winds through flat country alongside a canal. We encounter straggling little towns, red tiled and peeling plaster. Classical villas in their grounds, haymaking (still!) and shaggy bushes. Padua is modern blocks and traffic. Press on to Vicenza. The Basilica by Palladio is wonderful, and the Teatro Olimpico is way more interesting than imagined from reading about it. The Chiericati Palace is shrouded in matting but its forms still impress. Casa Palladio is a little gem. Sitting outside the Basilica, we chat with Yanks and an Italian who was a prisoner of war in Norwich. We eat spaghetti with wine at Trattoria Bella Vicenza. Sleep out in a hollow on a hill overlooking the Villa Rotonda.

John: Probably the "poshest" place I have ever slept in my life, but unfortunately not inside, was Palladio's Villa Capra "La Rotonda" near to Vicenza in Italy. A super simple building that paved the way for so many copycat buildings around the world. I dined out with my architectural friends for years after my boasting on this highpoint in my life. As it became my first night sleeping outside without a tent, I used the best of my knowhow to choose a suitable location - not liable to significant rainwater runoff, some low growth around to minimise horizontal air movement, growth over to minimise colder air dropping on us later in the night, not obviously visible thereby avoiding being moved on (this was pretty unlikely in Italy in 1964), etc. The darkening of the sky, the stars, sleep, the slow return to daylight was all so different from Venice - but both were blissful.

Vicenza: Loggia del Capitanio (JT)

Leon: The Villa was closed for restorations and from where we slept and woke, we succumbed entirely to Palladio's drawn and published ideal of 'bi-lateral symmetry'. In a lovely piece of sleuthing, architectural historian Andrew Hopkins points out (see NEITHER PERFECT NOR IDEAL: Changing mindsets at the villa Rotonda (forthcoming) 2021) that while the original design may have been for a 'casino' - a place for holding parties - the brief changed, and other architects completed the project making internal and external changes. Internally the four triangular newel post staircases snuck into the spaces where the central cylinder of space is reconciled with the square in which it sits were partly replaced with open centre 'a lumacha' oval stairs (designed by Vincenza Scamozzi) that reduced the width of the surrounding corridors. Windows were added to light bedrooms on the uppermost level. Externally the plinth, under-croft and the wide stairs were redesigned and purposed for the needs of a farm, and a falling away down the hill to the entrance, a colonnaded *barchessa* (barns and stables) was added. The four facades address different conditions: river and road / fields / woods / entrance (and barchessa). Innocent of these subtleties and still believing in Palladio's ideal, we made our way into the city for our morning coffee, overlooking the Basilica Palladiana (1546-).

Vicenza: The Basilica by Palladio (LvS)

DAY 60
SATURDAY JULY 04
TO THE PO VALLEY

Woken by a herd of dairy cows. In town we find the Loggia del Capitano and the Loggia Valmarana just as in the photos that we have studied. Breakfast on seven peaches and a half litre of milk each, for 100 Lire each! Scrumptious. It dawns on us how extraordinary it was to wake on the hill overlooking Rotonda! The tower of Porta Castello must be the model for Gio Ponti's Pirelli Tower in Milan (1956–1960). The shopping streets are colonnaded. There is some simple modern architecture using screens. Views through the arched doorways of many palazzi continue to entice with glimpses of wrought iron, wistaria, roses. We explore the brick vaulted Basilica thoroughly. There is a stall selling truffles. We lunch on spaghetti and wine again. Pass the faded Palazzo Angaran and cycle on to the Villa Rotonda standing self-sufficient on its hill surrounded by vineyards. We can't get in, it's under restoration. Statues are stuck nonchalantly to the pediments and there are workmen on the dome, only visible as such when they move.

We cycle to Este now in Italian countryside, hills pricked with pencil pines, or crowned with buildings. Foliage along the irrigation channels beside the road is rich yellow green. There are wheat fields freshly threshed, faded barns and farmhouses and more straggling dusty towns with classical fronted churches, and threshing grounds filled with clattering and dust rising as workers process the wheat. Then there are Plane trees along the road and big drops of rain fall.

Cycling now feels like the end of a cross-country race, not so far to go now, why not give in? But we don't. Love the dusty tracks leading to villas behind their crumbling walls, wrought iron gates. It is "Amadeo" country that inspired my first Italian love. From Este we enter the lush crop country of the Po Valley. There are ranks of Poplar trees, dusty roads, workers tending vegetable crops, tall maize, petunias, irrigation channels. Much modernisation: new houses, tractors, huge new barns. In between are crumbling farmyards with hens and the whiff of hay as it is forked onto a wagon yoked to two white oxen. How difficult it is to break away from Italians once you start talking to them! They love talking to foreigners. We reach Baruchella at 8PM, urns set up on the pavement, people playing cards, wandering in and out of the church. On to Bagnolla Po, small farms. The smell of thick powdered dust on the road reminds me of Africa. We sleep under a spreading grapevine and under a sky patterned black. It's all worth it!

Vicenza: Porta Castello, model for Gio Ponti's Pirelli Tower? (LvS)

John: As part of building up to contribute to this book, in no particular order I had written a list of "Great Moments" I always remember when thinking about Trip64 and didn't want to leave out. "Arrival in Venice", that I have covered above, was my 1st "Great Moment" and now for the 2nd – the "Po Valley". Locked in my memory is that the Po valley was a vast area of dirt tracks and dusty roads, with tiny villages, a few big houses and the odd town en route. I think we must have used the sun to guide us generally in the right direction to the next place actually marked on the map, because many roads/tracks were not marked on our comprehensive 1961 Touring Club Italiano map that I had bought in Stanford's, London before leaving home. It was basically an agricultural area, and time passed very slowly. It was almost like stepping into a different world and it made me feel I should behave or think differently. When it was becoming dark we found some vines to sleep under. I slept fitfully, partly because I was more interested in watching the electric storm slowly passing over us from north to south and waiting to see if rain would start, which it eventually did. I felt as though I would be happy to live here for the rest of my life.

Ravenna: Inside the Basilica di San Vitale (LvS)

DAY 61
SUNDAY JULY 05
TO RAVENNA

Woken by the sound of rain on leaves. John looks blue from copper sulphate run-off. I must too. We cycle in the half-light along dirt roads through farms. In drizzle and dark, stop at a small dark cafe alongside a canal in Runzi where we join farmworkers sheltering, gambling till the rain passes. They are drinking Aquavit. We settle on Vino Dolce and dunk our rolls.

> John: At first light we pressed on and very soon saw a small black shack with the odd slither of light coming from inside. What was it? As we got closer we heard men chatting to one another and the odd outburst of laughter – we had to see if we could join in. There was little spare room inside, but we were welcomed to join in drinking what was a strong alcoholic substance and nibbling small, sweet sponges. It was a magical experience for me, and I think also for Leon. The men gradually left heading for the fields and we left to get back on our, by then, wobbly bikes and head back into the 20th century.

There is a downpour. In eerie light we cycle to Ferrara, industrial and with a castle over-topped with towers. The fields are flat. At Argenta we stop and shelter for two hours in the Lancia garage, eating rolls and Nutella.

> Leon: Nutella became a staple from here on, and I have not been able to stomach it since.
> John: The pumpernickel and black treacle, for me, in the same way

Change out of wet jeans into shorts. We slog on to Ravenna in humid heat and rain, passing peach farms and – at a stall – we buy peaches. Lucious! The town is spread out on a flat plain. We find a hostel style place (Locanda Del Melarancio) and book in for an early night. Sleep like logs.

Ravenna: Piazza del Popolo (JT)

DAY 62
MONDAY JULY 06
RAVENNA

We buy a guide near the main square which, says the guide, has a "Venetian Palace" with "Venetian columns." Not quite, we think. We start at the Basilica San Vitale with its mosaics of Emperor and Empress Justinian and Theodora. The overall patterning is extraordinary, and the Empress is studded with gems. Folds in garments are shaded in but hang straight down. There is no perspective and no volume, but bare parts of figures are slightly modelled. The foreground is a stepped-up array of plants and clouds. The background is gold. The surface is gloriously surface, going up the dome and around into the apse, dissolving all sense of structure. The column capitals have a weighty top and taper down into carved away honey combed delicacy. Thus, the columns seem to hang from the dome. In the mosaic of Abel and Melchizedek there is an attempt at perspective, but quite flattened. Abel, a fair way into the apse, is nude. The Apostles are in an arc at the end of the apse. Christ is foreshortened into sitting position, the robe floating around his neck making a blue circle. Eyeballs in fixed positions, Abraham prepares to sacrifice Isaac. Chins are heavily shaded in. There is some quartering up of mosaics giving a Rorschach Inkblot look. Arches, arches.

John: I was struck with the Basilica of San Vitale having such a very strange plan form, nothing like I could remember in northern Europe, although during my subsequent career related and other travels around the world I of course saw many religious buildings in a different format from standard cruciform plans in England. This building got me into drawing plans and the odd detail of this and other buildings for a while, which I dropped quite quickly to concentrate on 3 dimensions. What San Vitale did do for me on a permanent basis was to make me try to draw volumes correctly and in perspective rather than in plan and elevation. Just the job for my future career in architecture. I found it hard to start with, but the result was that my drawing of the exterior of San Vitale was possibly my first and best ever (until then) 3-dimensional drawing of a building I had done. Due to the plan creating unexpected alignments, or should I say non-alignments, between certain external building elements, my drawing in part does not look accurate, but it is - I took a photo from the same spot as I did the drawing, and they are almost identical.

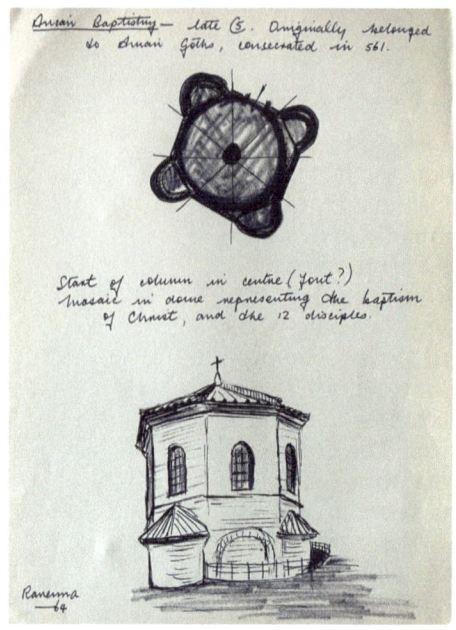
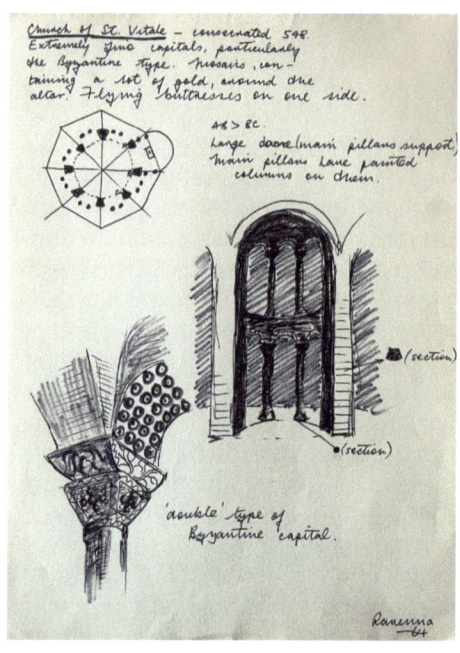

(above) Ravenna: Studies of Arian Baptistry and Basilica di San Vitale (JT)
(below) Ravenna: Basilica di San Vitale (Leon in the photo) (JT)

Then we go to Gallia Placida. Light glows through the golden grain of alabaster panels.

> Leon: The like of which I did not see again until visiting Gordon Bunshaft's Beinecke Rare Book Library at Yale in 1994.

There is surface-clinging blue mosaic. Birds in the foreground and on fountains. The Apostles, hands collapsed in a pattern, clad in decorative folds, flat but are arrayed in an illusion of space. Flames add a line of patterning, as do sheep. In the main dome winged symbols are afloat in a starry sky. The tomb is made of huge blocks.

> John: I think it was in Ravenna that I was really struck that the world is full of endless solutions to create an enclosed space, but all of them have the three same elements that we call floor, wall and roof. I had not even scratched the surface yet of looking at and understanding work by others as well as doing my own thing. I have already talked about the Basilica of San Vitale (6th century), but when I also experienced, in the same town, the Galla Placidia Mausoleum and the Arian Baptistry (both 5th century), I realised I needed to get my skates on to make any inroads into the art of architectural design and the construction that hopefully follows. Another layer of activity that also follows, is material selection – it was interesting to see that the Mausoleum uses thin marble instead of good old Pilkington glass to glaze the windows!

The Arian Baptistry is a small brick building in a car park. We go down steps and enter, finding ourselves under a great mosaic lined octagonal base dome. Bright rich colours contrast with the simple brick walls. Light comes in through arched windows in small alcoves. There is a pattern of Apostle symbols, and Christ is flat behind a blue line depicting water. St John is there with his stream and a Dove of Peace. Sandalled feet dangle in a repetitive frieze patterned with leaves. Foliage sits on poles between the ever-circling apostles, their expressions fixed. Flowers are shaded from red fringes to a white centre. Three sides of an altar are depicted. Christ alone is modelled, one arm in front, one behind. Stunning overall patterning!

The light flooded and simple nave with arcaded side aisles of the Basilica Apollinare Nuova comes next. Mosaics above the colonnades. Martyrs in series, sandalled feet, crowns and barley sugar poles and palm fronds between them. They march down to a seated Christ floating on a cushion, angels in attendance. Above this layer is a chequer pattern of windows, figures, scenes from the life of . . ., a cupola and doves. Side

Ravenna: Basilica di Sant'Apollinare Nuovo (JT)

chapels are baroque. The ceiling is coffered. On the other side there are seried virgins with crowns, some held forward, some to the rear. Sheep and plants surround one virgin. They process to a Madonna and Child, with attendant angels. The Three Kings arrive and seen through an arch are a sea dotted with ships and an architecturally fanciful port and the roofs of houses. The Three Kings are in Egyptian profile, legs astride, feet and hands in a flat pattern. Pattern, pattern, surface. Outside in the cloisters an old woman sells cards. The foursquare facade flows on arches to a brick tower punctured against the light.

    Back at the hostel the gravel is being swept. We sit out chatting to some Swedes and a couple with a baby and a Fiat Topolino.

```
DAY 63
TUESDAY JULY 07
RAVENNA TO PORTI DI KI
```

Make our way struggling across tramlines, past tired buildings, gas stations and pylons, to S. Apollinare in Classe.

```
Leon:      Michelangelo Antonioni's film Red Desert (which I
           loved), released in 1964 and starring Monica Vitti,
           had been filmed in and around Ravenna and Classis
           not long before we encountered its strange mix of
           ancient heritage and industrial landscape. Doing this
           transcript inspired me to read Judith Herrin, Ravenna:
           Capital of Empire, Crucible of Europe, Allen Lane,
           2020, London. She explains how Ravenna, situated
           amidst marshes and lakes at the mouth of the Po was
           closely linked to its port Classis, and this function,
           then as now, forged the city.
```

Inside there is a terrific form fitting skin of mosaics. Asymmetrical rocks are strewn about, sheep loom in the foreground. Archangels in patterned robes fill the apse finely balanced with the spaces between them.

```
Leon:      I can hear our art master telling us to draw the space
           between.
John:      Yes indeed Leon, but an axiom I often use these days
           when trying to guide Annie in the garden, is "a space
           does not exist unless there is something in it".
```

Each tree differs from the next, their bark heavily moulded. Flat mosaic pilasters between windows. A hand points from the clouds. Bigger bits of marble are used for stud patterning. Pale green shadows under the standing saints. Sheep are modelled by shading, but their feet are in a straight line. There are winged symbols of the Apostles. Moses has half his body in most un-cloudlike straggles of mist, picked out in red or blue with white shading. The basilica form with its long nave flanked by arches on columns gives emphasis to the altar's blast of splendour; Christ framed by the arch and centred by a cross and a disc. There are sarcophagi carved with symbols. The floor, once mosaic, is now mainly reddish tile. Pattern triumphs of realism everywhere. Sheep climb the hill on the sides of the segmented dome at the crossing. The gold mosaic here is speckled with brown. It sparkles.

On the way back to the hostel, John collects his money: one thousand! Yippee! We celebrate with gelati. Then we visit Dante's tomb, because it is there ... The Basilica of San Francesco (c.450) has a plain, mosaic free interior. The ceiling is a fascinating assembly of blocks squared in paint. The rafters are stepped up. Coins thrown into the crypt are rusting. Candles are L1000. Mass is celebrated. Outside we pass

through sterile modern squares to the Neon Baptistry; over decorated, it pales in comparison to the simplicity of the Arian Baptistry. A caretaker demands money. The brick mass of the Duomo looms above. It is time to leave.

We have Pizza Margherita and Vino rosso at the 'Touriste Cafe'. Return to the hostel to pack and to rest. Then we get going, which feels good! Even though the town and countryside are oppressive. Not what I expected. I loved the Po Valley, its lush vegetable growth and the eerie ride through dawn rain on the splashy gravel road. But Ravenna! The mosaics are fascinating, but town has a plastic ordinariness about it.

The road follows a canal and branches into a long diversion as the scenery grows increasingly varied. Peasant houses, crumbling villas, threshing yards – all make a continuous thread in time back to Byron (who "sung Ravenna forests" according to my guidebook), to Dante. I think, mind wandering, wheel spinning, tarmac flashing, trees passing. of Laurie Lee's travels in Spain: did it feel threadbare to him at times? Did he feel the call of home, even as he strove for independence? Did he feel lonely at first? My reveries are philosophical and then existential. What does the future hold? If all that is planned fails, are there other possibilities? Suddenly it strikes me that I am 19 years old, soon to be 20. I'm old! I have a debt to my parents and to my teachers.

The threatening storm passes, and mountain ranges now rise blue behind pines as we approach Forli. I have diarrhoea. A family allows me to use their WC. Forli is bleakly out of the Ferrara and Ravenna mould. Industry, tram lines, wires, bits of crumbling wall. Cypresses and weeds. Tourist bars. Reveries continue as we pedal pump the heavily laden bikes towards the hills. A girl in black bulges stands on a lawn. What about marriage? It is expected. At eye level are blue sprayed vines, cropped and cross bundled wheat, wet from recent rain, glowing in the sun. We freewheel down into the brick and tile mass of a fortified village. Arched upper corners of the castle overhang its corners. There is the sweet smell of sewage. We continue through trees to Castrocaro. Split levels, evening drinks on pavements, children playing in streets, hills topped with castles, the brick-piles of which are cut into with the black cut-outs of semi-circular windows. The foothills close in as we cycle alongside a winding mountain stream. Overlooking a white church tower, we eat white bread and Nutella. As we cycle on people shout out greetings and wish us good luck on the climb! I am lost in reverie. I had forgotten how the spatulate flanks of foothills are made to move by slanting evening light. How the creeping shadows of trees

Late evening nearing the summit of the Apennines heading for
Florence, ride halted by John's ball bearing drop and night fall
(JT)

make womb-like tunnels, contrasting with the dappled texture terraces of grapevines.

John: We had ducked out of cycling from Salzburg to Venice over a fairly narrow part at the eastern end of the Alps, but here we were taking on the Apennines full frontal. Obviously less of a huge mountain range, but a mountain range none the less, running most of the length of Italy, much like the Pennines in England, but higher. We wound up and through the foothills, stopping for plenty of fuel (food and drink) at roadside cafes as we went. The steepness of the roads increased. It was great to be off flat countryside, but hard going since the bike I was riding I had built myself off a heavy steel frame from a scrap yard, and I had removed the derailleur gears I had originally fitted from the bike before leaving home to avoid their potential failure – therefore I only had 1 gear for all terrains.

As we rise, towns are clustered into valleys, sometimes reached by flying viaducts. We cycle above, in, through the swooping levels, excited! Trudge, trudge, we pedal upwards. Under our arms we glimpse the plain behind closing, and looking forward, the ranges approaching. There is ear-splitting hooting at every blind corner. Far below stone and tile farmhouses seem to snuggle into valleys, folding in with them their hayfields, their cropped paddocks and vineyards. The orchards, seen from above, their canopies in plan, seem to flow their foliage along the road. In, out and around we swoop, the road hugging a contour, edging always upwards. The light is being shut out; a red sky appears in the groove ahead. Golden streaks stream across cooling damp shade. We stop at a trattoria in a hamlet. It is crammed with laughter and talk. Groceries on shelves, a gleaming espresso machine. The daughter of the establishment is being paid court while she reads a duplicated news sheet.

We press on. We see places under hedges where we could sleep. We want to spend this night under the stars. Now it is dark, the red glow has gone. There are lights in the windows of farmhouses. There is a cold breeze when we freewheel. We change from our shorts into our full gear. It is steep, we push our bikes, headlights beaming forward. Near Porti di Ki there is another Trattoria where we are welcomed by the proprietor and a young man. Drinking espresso, we chat about 'Mods and Rockers in Londra.' We watch Gregory Peck transposed into Italian, the locals grunt and mumble comments in unison. We drink Vino Rosso and in the half dark we are offered and decline cigarettes. At the end of the film,

we set out again having purchased a large lump of (cooking?) chocolate. Arrivederci! We find a place for our planned vigil, wrap ourselves in our sleeping bags and lie there raked by the lights of passing trucks, the barking of air brakes, heads in the weeds, smelling the bitter dew. I watch a spider spinning above me. The stars are close and huge, the Milky Way shimmers. We chat quietly, sharing associations between this night and nights of our childhood, mine in the Natal midlands and the Drakensberg foothills. I talk of my love for England, of Hedsor Lodge, of Cornwall, the moors, our school. I compare my distant connection to South Africa with the more intimate ones of the Couzyns. The breeze chills, I can feel the ground cold seeping into me, the dew forms heavily about us. We wait for morning.

John: As the evening had worn on the gradients increased and we had to stand on our peddles to keep moving. This was rewarded by getting a slightly better view over the beautiful, inclined countryside we were passing through. We started looking for a suitable place to sleep out under the stars. I then realised there was something going wrong with my bike down below – another one of my "Great Moments" is about to be revealed. I looked down and could see ball bearings falling out of the bottom bracket (the place where the shaft holding the peddles passes through the bike frame). The bearings were rolling off down the road and into oblivion. We stopped and luckily we found a suitable place for the night nearby to where we had got to. Mainly due to the lower temperature up in the mountains we got very little sleep, but it didn't matter for me as I was too excited about reaching the summit, which was not far away, and then swooping down the other side towards Florence.

Reaching the summit of the Apennines and seeing the road down to Florence - the site of a lorry hitting John (JT)

DAY 64
WEDNESDAY JULY 08
PORTO DI KI TO FLORENCE

John: Once it had become light enough, I checked my bottom bracket and found it to be partially unscrewed, presumably due to my standing on the pedals for so long to keep moving uphill the evening before. Not surprisingly I didn't have any spare ball bearings to replace those that had dropped out, so I tightened things up and off we went pushing for the top in the rising sun and the early morning clouds hanging in valleys below us. As far as I can remember, I never did replace my lost balls. Needless to say, another one of my "Great Moments" was about to unfold. We cycled or pushed for a while and then there it all was – a wide open sunny vista with some cloud below us, lower peaks and the road zigzagging down to civilisation and Florence.

The stars recede slowly, the hills vary in tone. Chilled in the dewy bags we get up and walk around, and then, muscles creaking, start pushing the bikes uphill away from the yellow light creeping around the long slither of the moon. The sound of our gears ticking we see as more and more grows into light. A rushing river splatters down the mountain flank into a pile of moss and then runs under the road onto tree clad precipices. We sit on roadworks drums and watch the sunrise in the valley. Eat Nutella and bread as early morning trucks grind by. On we go in the lung-chilling air. The sun is now streaming into the valley, leaving pools of shade, selecting and highlighting flanks and ridges, sparkling the wet, flower scattered grass. Rivulets gurgle down cold. Farms stir. In the white plaster, tucked under cliff houses, doors squeak, milk urns clank. Feeling the sun on my back, it's all sense and sensuousness: the road rises up and around paths running through mown fields and small orchards and past wooden spliced sheds to the river below. It is cool in the shaded bends. A woman in a doorway stares and then smiles. Pack donkeys file past carrying wood. Bon Giorno! Comes a greeting from behind as we snake down around a curve. It reminds me of early morning walks in the berg and returns over wet grass to bowls of oatmeal porridge. I long to be here forever, a stone that sees this always. At the top of the pass above the cool, hazy, morning-filled valley, we sit sunbaking. Looking down onto a rough tiled farm, a scarred hill and a boy walking up from a pond, we breath it all in.

Over the ridge we see stubby mountains rising out of a milk plain of cloud. Cappuccino and bread. Puncture. We are quiet.

Even if all the cycling had been agony, this morning would have made it worthwhile. We set off down in a hairpin winding rush, hands clamped to the brakes until they hurt, rims getting hot.

> John: It was then downhill for miles, braking much of the time and even more around the endless hairpin bends. Because of the hairpins we were travelling much of the time at a similar speed to the enormous twin and sometimes triple trailered lorries. On one stretch between hairpins, luckily when I was on the rising hill side of the road with a kerb a little way out from the hill-retaining wall, the last trailer of a lorry clipped my left shoulder as it swerved past resulting in my whole ensemble getting even closer to the retaining wall. My pedal scraped along the face of the kerb and my right shoulder along the rough stone retaining wall above for probably 30 metres before coming to a stop. Gosh that hurt, but at least I wasn't dead as I could so easily have been! A quick patch up and I was on my way again.

I seem to be seeing so many things that I had merely looked at before. How rocks jut out of fields, how moving light models the land. Terraces with only their fronts in shade reveal the shape of the mountain. Water falls from rocky ledges into the flat surfaces of pools. Trees massed on a hill each have their own shadow, and a shadow's shadow too. Paths fight contours as they rise up to glades. I see this, and I see what I had seen as a child. Then we are out of the pass and into the hills of Tuscany, winding through straggling pastel villages. The hills are stubbled with olive trees, leaves so light they seem to be reflected light.

Drunk on the seeing, exhilarated by freewheeling we sing "Quando, quando, quando!" (Wikipedia: 'an Italian pop song from 1962, in the bossa nova style, with music written by Tony Renis and lyrics by Alberto Testa.') People smile. We hurtle into a town entering at three storeys up over a double arch bridge with waist high balustrade below which we see a muddy trickle. On, down along the brown earthy River Arno to Florence. We stop for milk and bargain over the price, arms flapping. I see an Austin Van Den Plas. The cypresses on the surrounding hills shimmer in a heat haze. A glimpse of the Duomo: that dome! We see villas and an outstep tower. Dry, hot Tuscany. Through hot and earthy outskirts, we come to the hostel in a dry Italian garden. There is the usual ritual of checking in, then a hot shower, clothes washing, journal writing and a doze. We have a good hostel meal: chicken. Chat to a Dutch couple. Sleep.

> John: Florence was my most loved place visited on Trip64. I had briefly visited it before but more importantly

Florence: John sketching (LvS)

had subsequently studied quite a lot of the "famous" buildings there during my build up to taking my Art A-level exam. Much more would come while at university. The compact positioning of most of the "must visit and savour" places made me feel every time I went into the centre that I was drowning in great people's work and priceless visual experiences. On top of this, not only pleasuring visitors like me, but also the local population, was the way the normal things of life, like the rustic shops, bars, restaurants, sitting out places, etc. cradled all the "famous" bits. All of this imbrued in me a contentedness and peacefulness as I was sucked into the physical environment we found ourselves in. I have always thought this was a major contributor to why I produced many of the best drawings here in Florence on Trip64. I have been back to Florence on more than one occasion since 1964 and for me, sadly, it wasn't the same place as it was then. The centre is now very smart, containing many of the normal international chains of shops (like many other places) and is still very beautiful in many ways, but the contrast between great buildings surrounded by a rustic life has become less marked.

Florence: Duomo and Campanile (JT)

DAY 65
THURSDAY JULY 09
FLORENCE-1

Waking in a dormitory is depressingly un-private and underlines my sense of rootlessness. "Hello! Where have you been? How long are you staying? Where are you going? Who is next?" I want my own room! We walk down the drive to the bus. Jolt and crush to the Duomo. We walk the close streets with enticing shops and one room workshops, looking for milk. Excitement grows. In a city again! Where you can be rootless and yet have contact and imagine that passing girls – even cars – are for you. We buy a kilo of peaches – "Maturo!" – and, surrounded by statues and pigeons, we eat them on the steps of the Palazzo Della Signoria. Bite into the soft flesh and juice runs down tickling my chin and arm. In a bookshop full of art books in English and Italian, we purchase maps and guidebooks. Back to the Duomo, marble lined and quartered, the simplicity of the white with green lines of the Baptistry captivates. The Ghiberti doors with bronze panels using foreshortening and arcaded perspective achieve a three dimensionality in such a limited depth that I find remarkably intense.

> Leon: We were fortunate to see the doors before a flood in 1966 blackened them. When I next saw them in 2018, they had just been restored to their golden glory.

Ghiberti's groupings of people overshadow those of Pisano. Inside the Baptistry we marvel at Donatello's brittle wood carving of Magdalene, thrown into relief by light falling through the vast rising space. Fall in love with the floating marbles of Giotto's Campanile. Find the interior of the Duomo fussy but fun. Michelangelo's Deposition reveals how little is conveyed by photographs. For an age I explore this work with my pen, scoring in the movement, the grouping and the flowing space of this thing, so much a whole unto itself.

> John: My experience from travels in Italy prior to and during Trip64 showed me that the Italians had either an accidental or a deliberate skill in making you fight though lively streets and alleyways to reach that big building or space. In Rome the magic was destroyed by Mussolini's Fascist regime with regard to St Peter's Square, in Sienna it survived for its wonderful dished central "square", but in Florence it had survived big time around the Duomo and the two related buildings (Baptistry and Campanile). Not only did we enjoy the enclosure by generally basic vernacular buildings, but also the extreme difference in colour and texture between the Duomo Baptistry Campanile group (to quote

(above l.) Florence: Baptistry and (above r.) Florence: Duomo (JT)
(below) Florence: Palazzo Vecchio with Michelangelo's David, shot
from loggia off Piazza della Signoria (JT)

> Leon) and the surrounding buildings. At the other end
> of the scale, it was a delight that this was made fun
> of when after a long and tortuous climb to the cupola
> on top of the central dome of the Duomo, including a
> traverse between the dome you look up to from inside
> and the one visible on the outside, you were able to
> buy a cold drink, postcard or souvenir – I wouldn't
> want to be the delivery boy!

In a small market tunnel, we lunch on Pizza calda, frites and a peach – 50 lire. Return to the Duomo Baptistry Campanile group, watching light reveal the plastic space delineated by the inscribed marble. Rouse ourselves from this reverie and wander along the shopping streets to the Ponte Vecchio, which we – leaning in the sun – then watch from the farther bank of the Arno. Three flung arches support the slab of the wall with its windows and triple arched central opening, revealing the colonnades that march up inside. Then we move on and sit watching the wings of the Uffizi run together, the Ponte Vecchio visible through arches at one end of the alley, the Palazzo Signoria's obtuse angle and its comically placed thrusting tower looking like a bad photograph at the other. Then we sit in the Loggia dei Lanzi (della Signoria) surrounded by sculptures of Romans and rape. Cellini's Perseus is silhouetted against Renaissance facades beyond and people wind between the statuary and the fountains.

John: Several visits and one long stay in the Loggia della Signoria (Loggia dei Lanzi to Leon – both are correct) created another of my "Great Moments" (in this case strictly ½ day). The Loggia, being where it was on the south side of the Piazza Signoria, provided a cool cocoon throughout the day as well as lots of sculptures to look at. One of the sculptures is a copy of Michelangelo's David, the original had once been there but is now in the Accademia Gallery. With the Piazza straight ahead – considered by many as the main square in town – Florence's Town Hall, the Palazzo Vecchio diagonally opposite to the right, the Uffizi gallery adjacent on the right and behind, beyond which the River Arno flows by, and to the left little streets crowding in, it provided a static bridgehead to watch the world passing by. My long stay, as I remember it, was spent sitting in the Loggia for almost the whole of a day doing very little except thinking and watching. I did do some drawing and photography, had the odd bite and drink in situ, but little else. The fact that I have thought of that day so many times since, I believe, helped to point me in the direction my life would take – except that I settled in France

Florence: Sketches of Hercules and Anteus and other Pollaiuolo works in the Museo Nazionale del Bargello (LvS)

>  rather than in Italy once my formal career had been
>  completed.

What a day! Brunelleschi's dome, Vasari's frescoes, the Medici palaces! Jolt back to the hostel where we meet again (first encountered at the hostel in Ravenna) a Hungarian couple touring in an aged Citroen, he bearded like Karl Marx, she petite. Supper is saltless white bread, sardines and vino. Sleep.

(above) Florence: Palazzo Vecchio's tower with Uffizi Gallery either side (JT)
(below) Florence: A peep at Brunelleschi's and Michelangelo's church of San Lorenzo at the end of a market street (JT)

DAY 66
FRIDAY JULY 10
FLORENCE-2

Woken in the dormitory by a wail: "Vittore! Vittore! I don't want to go to Venezia!" What a way to wake! The smell of drains assails. We must find other accommodation. Bus into the city. Walk down narrow streets through cork manufacturing workshops, art shops crammed with bits of Byzantium and old sculpts. John buys a drawing pad. We stumble upon the slice side slab of the Basilica San Lorenzo, a market backing onto the facade. Through a gaudy flapping tunnel, we find the Piazza Indipendenza and the Pension Serena. We book in. A room of our own for a few days!

San Lorenzo! The clearly expressed volume of the Chapel of The Princes soars above the market stalls angled and flapping in the wind. The red-tile dome standing above the narrow mud-coloured streets. In we go and find thick white columns peeling under the weight above. Guides booming their spiel lead parties around. Upstairs marble encrusts everything in ponderous pinks, reds and dark grey. The ceiling is slung with decoration, walls lean in, the floor leaps up. Great bulbous sarcophagi loom out above head height, effete lily-pose statues are dressed in metallic cloth. It's oppressive, screamingly inhuman. We take a corridor to the New Sacristy, tucked in behind the chapel and find the Laurentian Library. Cool bulging plaster and dark grey structural elements, a taut crisp and delightful design by Michelangelo. The statues slipping off their sarcophagi set off the delineation.

```
Leon:     Recent research has revealed how, when it did not
          fit the space, the original design was modified in
          a dialogue between the clerks of work on site and
          Michelangelo then in Rome, achieving some of its magic
          in the process. See also Hopkin's account of how the
          villa Rotondo is in fact the work of three architects.
```

Out again through the marbled bedlam of the basilica, through the market stalls and looking back we see the volume of the New Sacristy tucked against the Chapel, and its bleak rise of stairs from back of the canvas stalls, set against the plain dusty wall. Heat radiates. We make for the Sacristy and push through a creaking door, an airlock and on into the grey pillars and crisp arches rising to a flat ceiling coffered in gold with central rosettes. This is interrupted by a painted cupola. Michelangelo's design here is also taut, while the Old Sacristy is cluttered and more mellow. Through the cloisters to the Laurentian Library this time looking down the staircase. In the panelled and wooden ceilinged library there are reading

(above) Florence: Tops of the central dome of the Duomo and the Campanile seen from the Laurentian Library (JT)
(below) Florence: San Lorenzo (JT)

cases. The light coming in through the windows is harsh. Photostats of ancient documents are displayed. Leaving, there is a view of tiled roofs and the Duomo and the Campanile beyond. Walk through the cool and delicate cloisters, shaded yellow. There is a glimpse of the Prior's quarters. We leave through the Porter's Lodge.

In a street full of restaurants, we pass huge peasant breads and giant T-bone steaks. So enticing, but our meal at 500L is the sparse fare of a 'tourist's lunch'. We pass the Duomo cluster that is casting chequered shadows. Sit in the Piazza Signoria once again amidst sculptures, people and pigeons. While studying the Pieta, rain came ripping down. Back at the hostel, sitting on the verandah, we watched the rain fall on the villa studded hills, and supped on unsalted bread and sardines and wine. After the rain a soft light shines through olive groves. Sleep tired but thrilled with San Lorenzo. Names of artists buzzing through my dreams.

John: San Lorenzo and its surrounding streets I loved most out of all the areas in Florence we spent our time in. Although it is the biggest church in Florence, and while Michelangelo had planned marble external cladding similar to the Duomo, Baptistry, Campanile group, the cladding was never implemented. In areas the rough brickwork has protrusions to support the cladding, and that increases the lovely texture of the external envelope as well as decreasing the size of what would have been large areas of unbroken brickwork. It's this resulting rustic exterior that integrates the huge building, encompassing as it does the church as well as several other functions included in the building mass, into the much smaller scale buildings and market stalls clustered around it. I spent many happy hours lurking around and about the building with the normal folk of Florence, buying the odd snacks as well as photographing and drawing what I saw. One particular day I spent most of sketching the domes of the Duomo from the external first floor covered walkways of the Laurentian Library. Looking back to my times in Florence I remember in the market areas often looking at a beautifully tanned Italian woman exposing her breasts, supposedly in preparation for feeding the baby in her arms, but actually detracting mens' thoughts while she checked out their pockets for a handful of lire. This may or may not have been occurring in 1964.

Florence: San Lorenzo (JT)

DAY 67
SATURDAY JULY 11
FLORENCE-3

We move to the Pensione ... and walk to the Vecchi Palace and explore its courtyard. We spend the morning in the Uffizi, following our guidebook rigorously.

    Leon:      `A note in my journal reads 'see guidebook'. This I annotated but it is lost.`

Then we sit watching the Ponte Vecchio from the shade under the Uffizi connecting bridge. Walk to the New Market; observe its upward thrusting arches, stalls rising bay on bay, colour on colour, trinket on trinket, vendors, jostling tourists. We meet the Couzyns and chat briefly. Have spaghetti and Pastina al Brodo at a Jolly Cafe for 180 Lire! Spend the afternoon consolidating at the Uffizi, then trail through the medieval core of the city and erupt into the large sun-baked piazza dominated by the 1860s gothic revival marble front of the Basilica of Santa Croce. The spaces inside are vast, which is emphasized by the smallness of people standing at the bases of the columns. Spend ages looking at the frescoes by Giotto in one of the small transept chapels – heads grouped around a pillar isolated by damaged plasterwork. Grey, brown and off-white and minimal tone and line. Tear myself away to study a group around a prone figure on the other side of the chapel.

    Supper at the Jolly Cafe – spaghetti and minestrone this time. Walk back to the pensione through rushing Saturday evening shoppers. The winding streets are torched with neon lights and cars and people jostling. Wash and walk back in the twilight. The stalls around San Lorenzo are lit by bulbs hanging centrally, dancing in the breeze, and in one case shining pink through lingerie. Bags, hats, leather goods, jerseys – all spot lit individually in the gloom. Stalls begin to close. There is a glow in the sky above the Duomo. We make our way to it and buy coffee and lemon gelati for 100 Lire and sit on the white marble steps watching people and chatting.

    Leon:      `For many years, this is the gelati that I recall when Florence is mentioned. In 2018 Annacaterina Piras recreates the moment for me with a superb ice-cream from Grossis.`

The white Baptistry looming up as the light fades. Tourists peer at the Ghiberti doors in the dark. The horse drawn taxis leave. Back to the Pensione where we sleep blissfully on our inner-sprung mattresses!

    John:      `Following a hard day at the pit face of finding, touring, looking at, rubbing, trying to understand, being smitten by or rarely repulsed by, photographing,`

Florence: Time spent sketching around the Duomo (JT)

drawing and, in Leon's case, making notes about the huge range of panoramas, groups of buildings, individual buildings, interiors, galleries, etc. etc., the time always came to take a pause for a while. Then is when we used to find a quiet and shaded place to recover and take stock. Side streets, I found more often than not, were where to head for. I guess like in many cities in Italy and southern Europe, there was a distinct visual and environmental difference between main thoroughfares and side streets. The side street buildings, of course, were simpler and the vehicles trafficked most of the space between faces of the buildings either side. Sometimes there was a pavement, but it would be narrow. The depth of shops and cafés back from the street frontage was normally small and thus activity often spread onto the street. This is how I remember the café we often ate at since it was cheap, and which Leon records was the Jolly Café. It certainly deserved its name. After a few days the Jolly Café was like returning home from school to devour the dinner mum had prepared. I believe there were a few small tables balanced on a pavement only slightly bigger than the table plus some stools with a shelf adjacent facing into the café. There was nothing better for me than sitting at a little table I or we had grabbed, drinking one or several of those very strong espresso coffees with a water chaser, watching people passing by, covering my ears as one of the many young boys on tiny but very loud 50cc Moto Bellissima or the like motorbikes flashed past, and think of being at university, learning about architecture there and one day to be able to design and supervise the construction of buildings myself. At one visit to the Jolly Café I learnt how to make my favourite soup – minestrone. Sitting on one of the stools with the small shelf adjacent to place my plate on and watching the food prep and serving going on in front of me as I was eating my meal, I realised that the minestrone I was enjoying was little more than the plate scrapings from other peoples' unfinished soups, spaghettis and any of the other dishes available - just topped up from time to time with water/stock/a few fresh veg and herbs. How very sensible compared with our world today where food hygiene seems to be more important than food taste!

(above) Florence: Buildings by the river Arno, and the Ponte Vecchio across the quickly flowing river (JT)
(below) Florence: On the Ponte Vecchio (JT)

DAY 68
SUNDAY JULY 12
FLORENCE-4

Set out to explore the other bank of the Arno and walk through a sweet-smelling maze of buildings studded with the odd Renaissance Palace with its rising roof above overhanging eaves, smooth plaster rising to smoother, shutters. Dusty yellow ochre prevails. We cross the Ponte Vecchio, viewing from the central gap the bridges arcading off downstream, the buildings clustered on the banks. Then, through wildly clustered buildings to the tarmac desert in front of the yellow mass of the Palazzo Pitti. People in the ponderous and oppressive yard look like ants. At one side we enter the gallery viewing its fantastic collection of paintings, crammed into heavily decorated rooms, each one competing for attention, reflections from the light coming in through windows and tour parties led by shouting guides create a blur. Were these pictures collected for love? Did anyone ever look at them? Who could? We take note of what we can and leave out the side of the gallery and confront in the hard sunlight the shiny tummy of Cosimo de Medici's favourite dwarf riding a turtle (Morgante by Valerio Cioli 1599).

> John: In my experience of all cities with a river running through them, the nature of things on one bank is different from the one on the other side. Florence was no exception to this. The north side contains most of the "important" activities and buildings, whereas the south side is much more laid back and green. In Florence the Arno's two banks has quite a few bridges linking them, but the Ponte Vecchio is undoubtedly the top of my list. Just a stone's throw from the Uffizi and Piazza Signoria made it another great rest area, as well as a delightful route to the south bank. Much like the "Old London Bridge" that was replaced in the first half of the 19th century, the Ponte Vecchio is much smaller but is actually still there, has buildings along each side of the central walkway which were lock-up shops in 1964, selling fresh fruit and veg, meat, etc. but now I believe these are occupied by jewellers, art dealers, etc. It was another great people watching place. Over part of the central span of the tree spans forming the bridge structure you could get to either parapet to gaze down at the River Arno making its brown and noble way down stream.

We return to the Duomo, dwelling on the Palazzo di Parte Guelph with its hugely exaggerated overhanging eaves jutting out over the street and over adjacent buildings, and its

(above) Florence: Looking downstream to the Ponte Vecchio (JT)
(below) Florence: Basilica della Santissima Annunziata and Santa Croce (JT)

external stair with arched doorway. Round the corner we find the Palazzo Davanzati with its roof top loggia sitting on a hierarchically graduated facade with arched openings diminishing in size towards it. Almost by accident, get in and spend an amazing hour exploring the entrance hall, the courtyard spreading to the extremities of the building, columns supporting the upper floors that rise in balconies around three sides with the fourth being an open stair (now glazed). There are frescoed tapestries depicting trees, garlanded arches, birds and crests, rich dark floors, coffered timber ceilings, heavy wooden furniture, thick walls, arches, nooks and the overhanging balconies and studded shutters. Rough plaster and roughly hewn fireplaces are picked out by rays of light such as those you get in an empty lift shaft. Huge beds, unevenly angled rooms. There are Madonnas in cupboards. A majolica pot is echoed on the doors to an alcove cut into the thick wall. A chest has fantastically intricate wrought iron hinges, inches deep. There is a long seated wooden couch on a plinth. It must be a special open day because most of the people exploring are locals. Such luck!

Leon: The facade – 14 century – unites a grouping of earlier medieval tower homes. The interior was 'restored' by Elia Volpi, an antiquarian, in <his impression> of the original style. So, highly designed. No wonder we loved it!

We try the lasagne at the Jolly Cafe – 720 Lire with meat. A marvellous meal but way too expensive! Sit it off sitting in the Loggia Della Signoria amidst the crazy sculptures and get shat upon by pigeons. Walk to Oltroarno in the blazing heat, threading our winding way through shuttered tenements and, rising between blanketing walls, pass through an arch to climb stony stairs shaded by fir trees. We get glimpses back of the domes and towers of Florence moving progressively into relief. Reach a green shaded contour avenue and follow it getting snatches of Florence below. Come to hot marble steps and climb to the Romanesque arched and green inscribed white marble face of San Miniato al Monte. From here there is a view of red roofs between dusty Tuscan hills, the red dome of the Duomo towering above. The towers of the castle punctuate. Our eyes follow the curve of the much-bridged River Arno. There are modern slabs of flats further down and close at hand the hill flanks are studded with stone pines and villas.

John: In my mind, San Miniato pushed San Lorenzo hard for my best loved church in Florence. Much smaller in size, but not missing its external marble cladding, in its elevated position on the south bank of the River Arno,

Florence: Inside San Miniato and its west façade (JT)

further upstream from "down-town", it was the church's
location seemingly floating over Florence that got
to me. From the paved area in front of the church I
could easily pick out everything we had enjoyed so far
and the things still to enjoy. Above all the Duomo,
Baptistry, Campanile group stood out against the city
scape and distant hills, with the strange tower of the
Palazzo Vecchio over to the left. The church itself
was a delight - small but perfectly formed.

At first it is very dark inside the church and then an echoing of the facade arches along the aisles becomes visible. The nave is split level with arched supports and a view through to chapels in the half basement and to the presbytery above – a dynamic architecture created with simple elements. The ceiling is painted timber. In the vault there is a chapel with Della Robbia tondos. Looking back up I am struck by the pattern of chair backs against the light from the doors, the people in silhouette. We sit watching for a long time. Then out and down a leafy way to the Piazzale Michelangelo which affords another panorama of the city, which we enjoy with locals and tourists. We buy 'Gelati Motta' cones that look so tempting but disappoint. Steps take us back down into the tenements and eventually we come to the fantastically ridged blank front of San Lorenzo. Today, when we step in, all is quiet with people coming in and crossing themselves.

    Back in our room at the Pensione I look at my drawings and wonder where all these crammed experiences will go. Write to Mum and Dad. We sup on bread and water to make up for the expensive lunch. Sleep.

Florence: Looking down over Florence from San Miniato with the Arno and Ponte Vecchio showing well in the bottom photo (JT)

DAY 69
MONDAY JULY 13
FLORENCE-5

Walk to the Medici Palace, marvelling at the way these renaissance facades rise: a robust stone bench, roughly hewn stone, less rough, smooth and then the jutting eaves as a cornice to the street. Michelozzo's courtyard is delicate and friendly. Walk the yellow streets to the Bargello fortress with its peculiar thrusting tower. In the courtyard the sun runs a shadow play across the external staircase and the plaques on the walls. Struggle to differentiate between numerous sculpted renaissance bods but enjoy a crumbling bronze turkey by Gambognola. There seem to be so many Davids! Maybe it is interesting to see how the sculptors play with the upright figure, such a simple subject. My heart is not in the analysis!

On to the Church of Badia which has a wonderful honeycomb ceiling, the coffers seemingly feet deep. A gothic tower dusty and punctured with openings, rises from the cloister. Walk through more yellow ochre tenement lined streets corbelled with jutting out roofs and full of bars and craft workshops. Find the church of Orsanmichele, a puzzling building with four equal sides and an arch leaping away from halfway up. It looks what it is: a closed in loggia. Here, states the guidebook, the external sculpture is "important'. Circle warily the Donatello and Ghiberti. They are superb.

Spaghetti and Pane Brodo at the Jolly Café.

> Leon: Our unimaginative eating was all to do with our tiny budgets! In 2018 Annacaterina led me and my credit card to one culinary delight – from haute cuisine to regional peasant – after another.

Then we sit in the arches of the Ponte Vecchio watching the work of strengthening the foundations, and a dog trying to play with the workmen. On the opposite side of our arch sits a blonde couple drinking from a bottle of Chianti. Make our way through Oltrarno noting a corner of a block cutaway to allow for a fountain. Pass S. Spirito and a piazza with a few tired trees, the heat pouring off great blank walls and people eating deep in the coolth of a trattoria. Sit on the steps of Santa Maria del Carmine, waiting for it to open, watching boys playing ball, chatting to an American who is also waiting. It's cool but fussily baroque inside, but the frescoes by Masaccio are fabulous. Twist and turn in the little chapel to take in 'The Expulsion', 'Peter and the coin' and 'The Baptism'. I'd settle for the Giotto heads though!

Then to Santo Spirito where we note the grey pointing used by Brunelleschi and Polliallou's Sacristy. A little dull, but

(above) Florence: Santa Croce and streets around (JT)
(below) Florence: Santa Croce (JT)

there is a homely smell and a ticking clock. Crossing back over the Arno we pause in the breeze the river generates. Note the British Consulate. The town presses on the river. Arched over trees fold around a bend. Into the Via Tornabuoni, handsomely lined with renaissance buildings and housing smart fashion shops and bookshops. Sit on the base bench of a building while hard tanned and nasal American girls walk by. Our favourite San Lorenzo and its market interpose, and then we are in our capital 'r' Room. I sit and write. At seven we leave and wander the town, the market now lit up, bargaining in full swing at the neon lit stalls. Sitting on the Ponte Vecchio we watch the sun set pink on the river surface under the bridges. At Jolly Café again! Spaghetti, minestrone and Chianti. The staff are friendly now, the chap with the twinkling face, the cashier with whom we keep muddling our change – we are regulars. We seek out a chocolate and lemon cornetto at the Duomo complex, now glowing softly white. On the steps others are talking about Barry Goldwater, then the right-wing bogey. Feeling English, peaceful and content, we feel lucky. Walk back to our room through closing shops. Sleep knowing that tomorrow is our last day in Florence.

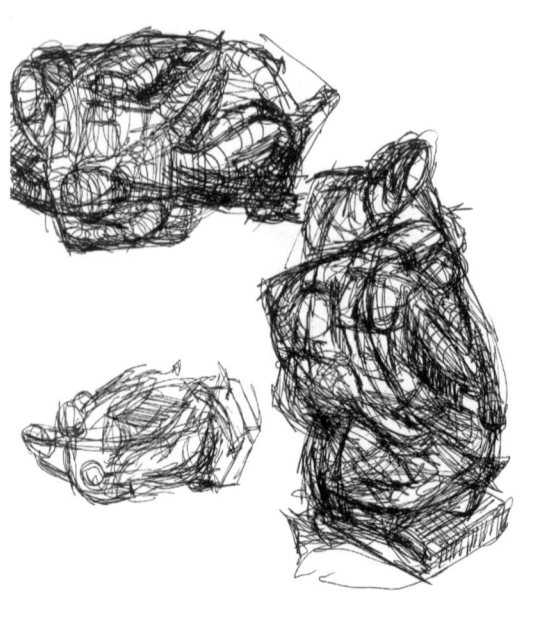

Heads isolated in repaired patch — grey & brown pale green background — fab. cluster. potter for space.

Simplicity of line, use of tone, overall design. Characteristic interpretation of face, fringe.

(above) Florence: The Deposition by Michelangelo {LvS}
(below) Florence: Giotto's frescoed heads (LvS)

DAY 70
TUESDAY JULY 14
FLORENCE-6

So much to see today! Penetrate through to the sacristy of San Marco to find the four semi-circular vaults of the library by Michelozzi. It's dark, smells homely and is hung with gowns and priestly duty rosters. One priest signs 'Oxonian'. The cloisters are graceful, yellow plastered. There is a panelled room behind the altar, very lived in. We continue to the Gallery of the Academy where we find a huge crowd queuing. I glimpse David through the door and feel that that is enough. Walk away from the tree filled and traffic whirling piazza to the Piazza Annunciata which is surrounded by Michelozzi's graceful porticos. Taut and light. The foundling hospital is a terracotta building with Della Robbia medallions. Make our way to the Duomo and on into the Church of S Annunciata where we find the Madonna of the Sack obscured by candles and worshippers.

    Enough gallery cramming! Done in the hopes that it is useful, but not finding direct connections outside the architectural wonders. Giotto's heads I am sure will haunt me, Masaccio's frescoes too. Michelangelo's sculptures always. For now, it's enough! Sit on the steps of the Foundling Hospital watching the street, roof eaves repeating, lights centrally hung disappearing under an arched corridor bridge. Reach through jutting eave streets the Duomo again, then down to San Lorenzo where I sit on the bench of the Medici Palace with John. The market bustling, while we observe the massing of that fabulous complex: the nave stark and simple, plummeting into the climbing volumes of the chapels. Later we head to Santa Maria Novella – and despite resolution earlier, study the Masaccio fresco of the Trinity and in front of a Lippi fresco depicting chaos sit talking until chased out by a man with keys. Then, enjoying talking and watching Florence pass by, we sit in the piazza in porticoed shade opposite the droop-shouldered facade, heat pouring down.

John:    Maybe be it was the lyrical flow of the name Santa Maria Novella, or that each word ends in an "a", or just happy memories of Trip64, I just don't know why, but during university and thereafter I often use that church's name to express my delight with something, relief after a near miss or as a swearword and all things between – the pronunciation and which word(s) receive the emphasis being tuned to reflect the use I am putting the name to.

Florence: Street scenes (JT)

The Jolly Café again, and spaghetti and pastina brodo. On the Via Tornabuoni we sit on a palace street base bench looking at a church smothered in reed matting and needing no analysis! English tourists have found their car parked in by scooters. At our room, we shower off the heat. Then in the evening we go to the spot lit market and on to photograph the Guelph and European Unity buildings.

Leon: Hard to grasp now in the age of digital recording how carefully we planned and rationed out our photographic shots!

At Jolly Café we have lasagne, minestrone and chianti, and bid farewell, explaining our journey in pidgin and sign language. We spend the rest of the twilight sitting with our backs to Giotto's' Campanile, our feet on the railings. We are in the midst of the marble complex, the simplicity of the Baptistry, the iced cake intricacy of the cathedral, the varied levels of the campanile. Have huge chocolate and lemon gelati cornettoes. Chat happily, sad to be leaving and yet it is time. A fabulous day, we agree.

John: After almost a full week of intense activity in this beautiful city of Florence I had run out of steam. I remember being somewhat relieved that tomorrow we would be back on the road and again heading into the unknown. I had taken a number of photographs (I had to limit the numbers to keep costs within my meagre budget) but had done a lot of good drawings that made me feel I had perhaps reached a peak in my drafting skills for the time being – I was very happy.

Pisa: Leaning Tower (JT)

DAY 71
WEDNESDAY JULY 15
TO PISA

We tear out of half-familiar Florence through the tenements that ring the city as semi-detached houses ring English cities. We swing on through parched towns, dusty villages, accompanied by the endless hooting of cars screaming past. We follow a muddy stream with lush reed banks, jagging up dusty Tuscan hills. In hamlets the shops and bars are all blank faced behind sticky plastic fly curtains. Even so we stop for groceries and find only cheese (very expensive), meat (also expensive and looking mouldy). Never much to choose from. Settle for sardines and bread. The heat bleaches and dries the landscape. In a factory yard there are stacks of green wine bottles. Some of these and clumps of raffia are being delivered to individual houses by handcart. Striking poverty and striking opulence here. Suppose the first step is to recognise the gap. Class is not even thought of, the distance is so vast.

Vines give little shade from the all-penetrating sun. There are occasional patches of delight: yellow green trees strung out above a terracotta wall; curves of a hill dotted with olive trees; a road rolling up to a farmstead. There is the odd building under construction, full of contemporary gimmicks that will crumble and rot. Towns are presaged by AGIP petrol stations. Now a midday lethargy has spread. People hang out at every bar, looking enervated and bored. The road rolls on. A tarmac rushing-under feeling lightens my mood. We whoosh through hills and come to a view of a flat plane below, dotted with red tiles houses. It looks hot, dry, dusty. Maybe drought stricken? We free wheel down into a yellow plastered town; tram lines appear above us – it is Pisa. We cross a river, lined orange and black, there is a piazza with drooping vegetation. A colonnaded street gives welcome shade. We glimpse a white marble facade beyond a high brick wall topped with a hedge, sweep round to the left and, my God! It leans! There behind a row of pencil pines is the crazy tower, set in meticulously groomed grass.

John: I had had lectures on the history of art and architecture as part of taking A-level Art (at a School of Art since our great art teacher at school, Robin Pitman, concentrated specifically on "creating art" by our production of drawings, paintings and sculptures) so I was not unfamiliar with the Leaning Tower and its associated buildings. I ground to a halt as soon as I found myself in what seemed to be a

Pisa: Baptistry (JT)

different world. It was wonderful to walk around and through the three buildings, experience the striking differences in shape and form, with their colour and texture, as well as the beautiful matching stone bollards, holding them together. I have to admit that the Baptistry was my favourite.

We buy Pepsi Colas and sit in the shade just looking at the Duomo, Baptistry and Tower as a set, vibrantly different to the untidy morning ride. The apse end of the cathedral is superb. Pulling on our jeans over our shorts to gain entry we go inside: a coffered ceiling supported by arch over arch sits over a double ambulatory. Admire the Giovanni Pisano pulpit. The egg dome above. The Baptistry has a round dome and a better pulpit by Nicolas Pisano. A cool pure volume. Tour guides bray into the echoing silence. Climb the tower, noting the arches match those of the Duomo. See a succession of people being photographed as if propping it up. Italian youths joshing each other. Dwell in the throng drinking more colas. Feel the wonder of it seeping in.

John: Having been in Florence for several days before, the penny dropped for me on arrival at the Duomo, Baptistry, Campanile group in Pisa. In northern Europe, the place housing the bells that call you to church, where you get baptised and later where you worship are normally arranged within the same structure. In this part of Italy at least, the three functions have their own building which I loved. Not only can "form follow function" be more positively implemented if you take the Italian route, but also the space between the three elements offers greater opportunities externally than just standing around outside the west door of a northern Europe equivalent before and after a service.

Having subsequently had a career of over 40yrs as an architect, mainly designing and supervising the construction of large public buildings in many parts of the world, I am now only too aware of the need to provide a safe environment for people to be in. I remember coming out from the central staircases core running up the campanile ("the leaning tower of Pisa") and walking around the ancient stone floor between the central core and the outer face of the building. Having climbed the nearly 300 uneven steps up the centre and been hit by the views when you get to the top, I wasn't prepared and forgot that the floor slopped so much and the balustrading I was heading for was either not there or, if it was, designed way below today's rules back then in 1964 – eek!

(above) Pisa: Baptistry, Duomo and LeaningTower (JT)
(below) Pisa: Sketch of Leaning Tower, Duomo and Camposanto (LvS)

Leave, holding an image of perfection in mind. Roar down the coast road lined with Stone Pines – all trunk and then spreading canopy. Sing (our theme song since Venice) "Imagine I'm in love with you / it's easy cos I know / I've imagined I'm in love with you / many, many times before. / It's not like me to pretend/ But I will get you in the end . . ." (Lennon/McCartney, the Beatles, 1963). Elated by the day we flash through Livorno (Leghorn on our English maps) noting industry, blocks of flats, potholed streets. Come to Victorian villas with loggias on their roofs, then big hotels: the coast road! It is lined with flowering shrubs. Up over a rise and we see the Mediterranean!

> John: The sea is actually not called the Mediterranean here – it's the Ligurian Sea which further south becomes the Tyrrhenian Sea and eventually the Mediterranean, but it seemed to be we had reached the "Med" after cycling most of the way from the "Channel"!

Blue and endless packed beaches and pebbly coves. On we cycle, on towards Rome! Eventually between the fenced off palaces of the rich we – sweat-encrusted – pass through a gap to a pine shaded beach and swim. "Non privata? Si." Clean, cool and feeling marvellous we eat bread and jam. Evening comes and the other beach users pack and go. The sun sets over the water, a red disk with a misty rim. Some late swimmers dry on rocks in silhouette. I write my journal. We pull out our sleeping bags, doze off to the slap of water against a fishing boat. Trains pass. There is a slushing of pebbles, the clunk of rolling rocks. Dream of family holidays in Cornwall.

> John: To impress girls during the years following Trip64, I used to brag about my heroic long-distance dash to Rome. My memory was always telling me that after our stop in Pisa we had arrived at the Ligurian Sea, tried to sleep on the beach but, due to huge numbers of biting insects, we had decided to head for Rome down the ancient Via Aurelia. That would have meant a single stage, with the odd sustenance stops, all the way from Florence to Rome. This really did the trick with most girls. But it seems from Leon's journal that we did have a sleep soon after we had reached the coast on Day 71. Also, from the journal it would appear that the night between Days 72 and 73 was when the insects (and a dog) got the better of us. However, what we did actually achieve should not be sniffed at and would still have done the trick with the girls. Having located where I think we may have slept during the night of Days 71/72, from setting off again early on Day 72 and arriving at the Albergo del Sol in Rome early evening on Day 73, we had cycled on clapped out

Pisa: Duomo seen past the Tower (JT)

heavy bikes, loaded with our worldly possessions, an incredible 293kms (183 miles) with just the odd doze on the way. How did we do it - it must have been all that time in the Borlase 1st Eight, building strength, stamina, determination, and comradeship that had prepared us for this rather unnecessary achievement!

DAY 72
THURSDAY JULY 16

Wake to the dawn, fishers still at it. How my father and I love early morning walks! As the first rays of sunshine reach our cove we swim in warmish, waveless water. Then make our way through the pines to a village for coffee, milk and a sweet roll, and provisions. Press on through the morning and into growing and grinding heat. It's the Via Aurelia! Straight and rolling, sometimes lined with pines, sometimes not. Despair at Roman lack of romanticism. We stop for water and cola at a grocer-bar between petrol stations, hot white country with stubbly hills on the horizon, the sea flat. "Roma?" we ask. "Due mezzogiorno" we are told. On we press, on! Traffic, lines of trees, tarmac; crop and crack country. We divert to Follonica Beach, waiting for a train to pass. Here there are big hotels, packed beaches and shady streets. We can go no further. We find a space below the sea wall near a sewage outlet and spend the rest of the day on the sand and in and out of the water. Eat sardines and bread, drink colas. All along the beach there are hot tanning bodies. This does not appeal to this heath, heather and mist lover not a sun soak and tanning oil type.

    We set off again through pines, and find 'aqua?' 'Si' at a bar. The road climbs a hill onto a promontory with a pleasant central valley of orchards. Peaches at stalls attended by a woman in black are 60 Lire per kilo. This poverty is horrid! We cross the outer rim through pines and dry pine litter and signs warning of fire. Down the other side in a great whoosh, the dry air tearing the liquid out of my mouth, which feels clogged. We pass through a belt of pines buzzing with cicada calls. Modern villas appear on the right, opulent cars in their driveways. Stop at a garage for aqua. Next is Castiglione della Pescaia, pleasant with buildings packed in against an inlet harbour sheltering the roaming rich. On through a 'pineta' – pine forest, taking a track inches deep in sand and cut through dunes to the sea.

Leon: In 1965 Fellini's film Juliet of the Spirits was released, and it seemed to me that we had been in the pine studded dunes that feature in the film

Dump our bikes, strip and roll across the cold wet sand into the sea. It is cold! Not lukewarm like the Lido! We revel in it. Then, sitting on the edge of wet sand, we eat bread, jam and peaches. Bathing parties disperse, the sea goes slush, slush. The intimacy of evening grows around us, Castiglioni outlined against hills that are seried blue on darker blue. The sun becomes a red disk. Lights sparkle in the hills, then the moonlight is faceted on the rippling sea. On the edge we try to

sleep, plagued by insects. I hear John's feet grinding in the sand, the sand groaning against waves, the water rolling back making a sound like rain on leaves. Swaddle up and doze a bit under the great open sky, the moon and the stars. I feel jealous of my independence, loath to go home, yet looking forward to that. In some way 'apron strings' have been cut. I feel apart, ready to work my way through life. Why not go back now? Ask for no more money and go straight to Lausanne, getting back in early August. No need to prove myself any further...

> John: Our long-distance ride down the Via Aurelia really was something for me at the time. The exhaustion, lack of sleep, resultant loss of logic, the heat even at night, periods of extreme hunger and thirst, hooting horns, biting insects, huge thunderous lorries and their trailers, a long period of darkness, a lonely dog, oases of light from headlights and mini service stations, getting closer to my life's goal of being a famous architect, all made me feel I must have arrived on that astral plane above earth. I must have been mad to keep going through the night following my near to death lorry experience while going down the Apennines towards Florence, and that was in broad daylight!

We retreat from the beach to a late-night garage bar and chat to Tony, the barman, a nice Dutch student on a working holiday. It's too hot to sleep. My eyes are bothering me. We chat to a girl from Ohio who supports Goldwater. This is all wrong! I have flipped in the heat. We try to sleep again but are woken by a dog, that having poked its nose into my back and then John's, is standing against the moon-yellow water. John walks off to get a cola. I finish the peaches paddling in the water. John returns and wordlessly we pack and set off through the pinetum dust, and pedal heavy-lidded down the provincial road.

DAY 73-80
FRIDAY JULY 17

Stop for tea at a bar and then press on through the night, eerie and unreal. The road is flat, and we are swept by lights from in front of us and from behind. Traffic streams along the potholed surface. We lose any sense of rising or falling, cross bridges and see no water, pass through pockets of cool air surrounded by hot breezes. Lorry fumes envelope us but the lorries carefully avoid us. We sit on a mound under a pine eating the last of our bread and jam. Dogs baying around us. Thrash on blindly, watching lights approach down an avenue of trees, splitting and then joining in an eye-dazzling blaze. The road becomes a chartless sea without edge. On and on through sleeping villages till yellow lights loom up and we cycle into the artificial day of an AGIP all night bar and drink cafe latte, suchi di frutta, tea, and eat pizza. Everyone seems bleary eyed. Lorries pull in, we glimpse the mates sleeping in bunks behind the driver. It's all passing, light begins to come into the sky, a milk lorry passes. We stop and are swarmed by insects from the hot grass. Check the map, on. The dawn grows pink above brown ploughed fields stubbled with yellow corn stalks. The country is bleached white, the dust is white, the olives are silver, the houses are yellow – the never ending Via Aurelia.

A medieval mess of a hill town appears, smelling sweet and sickening. We snatch food at another AGIP – coffee, tea, succha di frutta, tosti. On through the white countryside, rolling hills, crumbling walls powdered white broken by ruined elaborate wrought iron gates. Through a brick archway we glimpse a curve in the road through olives towards the sea, but we see no water beyond a pale beach. Pass through another medieval town, its serried towers moving in silhouette against the morning sun. There is a scrabble of petrol stations and new flats. Down and up the heat choking road past a regimental HQ – all feathers and salutes – and whizz in the hot breeze into Civitavecchia. We see derricks, a power station. Wheeling the bikes – I have a puncture – a man greets us: "We nearly won the war!" "Inglesi!" we retort. "Wonderful prisoner of war camps!" is his pause-less segue.

There is no beach to rest on, we push onto another AGIP, sort puncture, drink colas. Make for the sea across parched grass, rubbish and rocks. Collapse into a little bit of shade, soon gone. Signs warn against swimming. We struggle back to the road. There is no stopping for us. At last, after freewheeling giddily we find, in a resort village, a Trattoria. We eat a four-course meal, sweat pouring off us, suffocatingly loud music playing. We head off in a desperate search for

Rome: Sketch of view up the Tiber with Castel Angelo on the right (LvS)

shade. There is nothing but the hot, inescapable road buffeted by warm breezes. At last, we find a concrete ledge between a low and a high hedge, and lying on this, fall into a doze for an hour as traffic and trains surge past. Then drink tea in a hot bar, my head swirling with possible plans. We manhandle the bikes down to a beach and swim in the cold sea. The respite soon wears off and we set off again cycling in an endless heady eye-blaze, foot-thrash nightmare along the straight flat road to Rome. We stop only to ask for water, Rome in our sights, checking the stone kilometre markers, knowing only to get on. By now my mind is wandering, eyes burning, sweat pouring, and I have difficulty keeping the bike from swaying. Cars roar past and my head shrinks away from every hooting scream. Roma! Roma! Roma!

Coolth came late and with it the sight of an Alvis drophead coupe driven by a blonde man heading for the coast.

> Leon: My father's partner Maurice Lee had one of these supremely desirable cars – pale metallic blue with white leather seats, designed by Graber of Switzerland. For years I harboured a wish to hire some poor youth to cycle remorselessly towards Rome while I – in my Alvis – drifted past ignoring him!

Every stop meant new efforts to force the bike up to cruising speed. My mouth clogs and I taste seawater. But the hills become long and smooth, the road widens, the traffic flows, and we are cutting above white valleys with steep sides and flat bottoms. We pass no towns, no houses. A sign reads: "14km Roma". Yet, hill on head-thumping hill we can see no sign of the city. Till over one, there it lay! Rome! I could hold it in my hand. So, this is what a real city looks like! On, blurring past sprinklers spraying evening lawns, over uneven surfaces and in between blocks of flats John leads us to the Albergo del Sol where attempting normality, we book in.

I remember eating under a vine, then collapsing into bed.

> John: The daily journal entries generally stop here – just the odd one appears – mainly notes written after this point, but Leon's slides chronologically outlined our journey around Rome from the numbers printed on them:

01. View of small dome in Vatican garden
02. Ditto
03. missing
04. View of dome of St P from rear
05. Man drinking from ship fountain, Piazza di Spagna, Barcaccia Fountain (1627–9) attributed to Pietro Bernini
06. Twin cupolas facing Victor Emmanuel steps
07. Trevi?

Rome: St Peter's seen through columns of Bernini's Colonnade (JT)

08. View along Tiber to Castel Angelo
09. Spanish steps
10. Construction matting in a side streeterno
11. View down Via Torino to Santa Suzanna (1604) by Carlo Maderno
   Leon:     Church illustrated by Heinrich Wolflin in his book, Renaissance and Baroque, Collins, 1966, London E1
12. missing
13. missing
14. Blank
15. Piazza Navona
16. Gian Lorenzo Bernini fountain Fontana del Quattro Fiume, apocryphally – according to guides – the cowering figure of the Rio de la Plata river is appalled at Borromini's facade of Sant 'Agnese.
   Leon:     (Basil Richmond in my ear!)
17. Olympic stadium
18. Olympic village
19. Steps illustrated in Rasmussen's 'Experiencing Architecture'
20. Side street
21. The Colosseum
22. The Colosseum
23. The Arch of Titus, AD 81. Via Sacra, to SE of Roman Forum. Frieze of 'The Fall of Jerusalem'.
24. A fountain at night Trevi
25. Trevi at night
26. Blank
27. The Albergo with Leon
28. Leon drinking at a fountain, bikes of John and Leon visible
29. Leon and bike in front of St Peters
30. Stairs to the Campidoglio by Michelangelo, and stairs to Basilica Sancta Mariae Coeli in Capitolio, formerly the temple of Juno Moneta.
31. missing
32. missing
33. Fountain and stalls
34. Palazzo Massimo
35. A side street
36. Steps of Victor Emmanuel Memorial and cupolas of San Pietro in Vincoli and Santa Maria sopra Minerva
37. End of roll: VE steps and one cupola

Rome: Leon at St Peter's (JT)

Rome: John at St Peter's (LvS)

Rome: Palazzo Massimo (LvS)

Rome: Santa Maria di Loreto (JT)

(above) Rome: Santa Maria di Loreto (JT)
(below) Rome: Santa Maria Maggiore and Santa Maria di Loreto (JT)

Rome: Santa Maria Maggiore (JT)

(above) Rome: Sant'Agnese in Agone (JT)
(below) Rome: Basilica Parrocchiale Santa Maria del Popolo (JT)

(above) Rome: Bernini's Colonnade in front of St Peters and Colonna Traiana with Santissimo Nome di Maria al Foro Traiano (JT)
(below) Rome: roofline/building elements and people around town (JT)

Post trip drawing benefitting from John sketching in a pub in Cookham prior to the trip followed by sketching in lots of bars during the trip (JT)

Rome: Roof lines (JT)

(above) Rome: Leon drinking at a fountain, bikes of John and Leon visible (JT)
(below) Rome: Capitoline Hill (JT)

Rome: Capitoline Hill (JT)

Rome: Pantheon (JT)

DAY 73-80

Rome: Spanish Steps (JT)

(above) Rome: Barcaccia Fountain sited dangerously in the road at the bottom of the Spanish Steps, designed by Bernini, with Café Byron to right (JT)
(below) Rome: Stairs to the Campidoglio by Michelangelo and stairs to Basilica di Santa Maria in Ara Coeli in Capitolio, formerly temple of Juno (LvS)

Rome: Palazza Venezia (JT)

Rome: Trevi Fountain (JT)

Rome: Arch of Titus, AD 81, Via Sacra, to SE of Roman Forum (LvS)

Rome: The external face of the Colosseum (JT)

Rome: Interior of the Colosseum showing dungeons below the battle area (latter long gone) and support to the audience's seating (also long gone) (JT)

(above) Rome: Forum - Arch of Septimius Severus (JT)
(below) Rome: Forum - Baths of Caracalla (JT)

319      DAY 73-80

Rome: Forum, general view (JT)

Rome: Arch of Constantine (JT)

Rome: View down Via Torino to Santa Susanna (1604) by Carlo Maderno (LvS)

Rome: A back street (JT)

Rome: NBBS Hostel, home to Leon and John while in Rome (JT)

Leon: What follows is what I wrote in my journal number 2 for Day 74 <Saturday July 18> to Day 80 <Friday July 24 >

The Albergo del Sol became our home in Rome. That first night we absorbed that it was in an area of new blocks of flats and yet the motifs of the architecture we'd come to know permeated it. Yellow ochre plaster, irregular block layout, vine covered pergolas in gaps, shutters, the grey light of TVs in the windows, a stair rising through darkened windows. Our room was painted yellow.

   Striking images:
The moon rising above the Pantheon's floating portico; the cool sounds of fountains; walking through shaded streets freed from the weight of the sun; the white hulk of the Victor Emmanuel memorial; Michelangelo's broad steps rising – flowers and yellow foliage edged – to the Campidoglio and the stairs to Basilica Sancta Mariae Coeli in Capitolio at an angle; the rising volumes of churches expressed as block on block to thrusting dome; the grey of stone buildings above the yellow of the alleys; the fountain 'Fontana delle Api' (1644) for Pope Urban VIII Pont. Max., by Gian Lorenzo Bernini, nestled in its hole.

   Things we did:
Sitting in pavement cafes drinking coffee and eating flaky pastry, comfortable in the soft light and gentle warmth. Walking across the Tiber, the arches of the bridges cutting the arches of other bridges as the river bends; seeing Castelangelo light as a ship. Approaching St Peters obliquely rather than on axis; seeing the colonnade move around now silent fountains – the sound drowned out by people walking. The dome hovering grey and golden above, the cobbles revolving to the centre, couples isolated. The bus back to the albergo jolting, walking the streets now still. We open our bottle of chianti and drink some. Go out to find a pizza and find one at Righetti and eat it under the vine, talking and laughing, happy. Go to bed giggling and drown in sleep.

   Life begins in the evening:
The neighbourhood with its patches of flats and straggle of shuttered shops, dusty unmade pavements and a tarmac marketplace fills slowly with people. At first, they sit in the shade outside bars, playing cards. At the fountain a watermelon man begins to set out his stall, splitting ice, placing leaves on blocks, filling the fountain trough with green and pink slices. People gather and move on until the call goes

Rome: Nervi's Flaminio Stadium (JT)

out and the pink slices are placed on the ice and water drips from the table. "Venti! Venti! Bella! Bella!" Nearby a wooden stall dispenses fruit drinks. Children and parents move along munching their way to the supermarket. People pour off buses. A father arrives home to welcoming kids. The activity builds until darkness closes in and lights go on under the plane trees. People crush between the main stall and pavement chairs. Pips cover the ground. A matron buys a whole melon, watching the lever arm scale suspiciously and voicing her suspicion! A chorus of greetings and small children falling through adult legs. People are eating under the vine at Righetti's, and soon the flats are filled with lit windows and the street goes back to its roller shuttered state, leaving only men and us sipping wine.

### Day 4 in Rome
We explore Boulevard Rome – Trastevere. Vaguely renaissance blocks five to six storeys high line wide streets with jaggedly pruned plane trees. It has a grid layout, but the dusty yellow plaster is pervasive. There are views to the Tiber between parked cars and through the endless roar of the traffic. Newsstands colonize corners. In the side streets temporary markets sell peaches, bananas, figs, eggplant. Some stalls vend clothes. Chairs and tables spread from the mouths of bars. People sit sipping, reading, watching passers-by. There is a glimpse of a fountain.

### Day 5 in Rome
Small shops are built around their standard metal roller fronts, all the same size, only the lettering changes: Rosticierra, Macelleria, Copisteria, Bottigleria, Trattoria, Pasticceria, Pizzeria. Plastic tapes flap in all openings, big shops have two. They close in the heat and everyone retreats behind shutters and the buildings become faceless. The municipal market hall is cool, cries rise from the stalls piled around a fountain. People pour through, tourists are palpably ripped off!

### Day 6 in Rome
We seek out the Olympic stadiums, searching for the small one by Nervi. A big one is slung like a pot being thrown. We note the repetition of the grey concrete structure and the white infill panels, the hung perambulatory stair. There are views through; this is not an opaque building. It is cool under cover. The structure repeats in a flyover beyond which we see the long facades of the Olympic Village, orange and shuttered. We find the Nervi stadium with its coffered ceiling,

(above) Rome: Nervi's Palazzetto dello Sport (JT)
(below) Rome: Nervi's elevated motorway in the 1960 Olympic village (JT)

approaching between pompous statuary. No one with a sense of humour could have erected these!

John: One of the structures built for the Rome Olympics, held in the late summer of 1960 while I was at Borlase School and Leon was about to arrive, gave me a massive jolt when we visited the Olympic site. The Hammersmith flyover in west London had been built during 1960-61, an exciting structure to me for England, seemed to have been a copy of Nervi's flyover here. A similar structure was also emerging for the West Way, the initial part of the new A4 motorway linking London to Bristol and South Wales. Gosh, I thought, when I get through university and beyond will construction also have the copycats like there are at school!

Day 7 in Rome
We do the Piazza N and Bernini's fountain. We do the amphitheatre, we do the Spanish Steps, we do Trevi and photograph a man drinking from the fountain. We do the Appian Way. And so on from photos...

Rome: Railway Station (JT)

DAY 81
SATURDAY JULY 25

Leon: We did go to Lausanne. I wonder why it is out of John's memory.
John: I do remember that post Trip64 I did used to talk about stopping in Lausanne on the way home, but sadly I cannot remember being there.

**We leave on the train to Lausanne and the Swiss National Exposition, see Swiss National Exposition, Official Guide of the Swiss National Exhibition, 1964, Lausanne.**

(See Architectural Review in Leon's library: Davey, Peter, Lausanne Expo cxxxvi, The Architectural Review No.810, Architectural Press Ltd, August 1964, London).

## DAY 82
## SUNDAY JULY 26

Leon: And I remember us trying to sleep - shoulder to shoulder - on a night train to Paris.

**We pass through Paris on a night train, sleeping fitfully and cross the city to the boat train and Victoria Station.**

Journal number 1 ends in Venice. On the cover of journal number 2, which ends with us arriving at the Albergo del Sol on Friday July 17, there is this note:

**"12 weeks complete, last three not chronicled"**

This would take me (Leon) from 06 May to 29 July ... but accurate dating was not in my mind. I believe I got home during the first week of August.

## EARLY AUGUST

Leon: An awkward leave taking at Paddington? Or Victoria? Or Bourne End? - as it dawned on us that our joint project was over, and our divergent futures grabbed at us.

John: My bike had received serious tyre damage on its journey from Rome (or Lausanne) to London, making it unrideable when it was back in my hands at Victoria. My memory is that our "awkward leave taking" took place at Bourne End rail station. I then pushed my loaded bike up the lane to Flackwell Heath and home. It was about noon when I arrived and thus both my parents were at work, but not Mrs Fisher next door (mother of another Borlase School student), and I heard screaming as she realised that the dishevelled and bearded person walking past her was in fact me. I received a very welcome large glass of water and a real English tea!

# REFLECTIONS

JOHN

So, we made it home in one piece after a truly wonderful and memorable journey and one I look back on with great pleasure. What's more, excluding the train over the Alps, it was only to get to the summit of the Apennines that we had to get off our bikes and push. For me, it lived up to everything I had hoped for. It was founded on and a continuation of my life's development. But what happened next?

As Leon inferred in what he wrote right at the end of the Journal (under "Early August") a distance had begun to grow between us as we arrived back in England, or perhaps earlier. Was it simply because we had had an unbroken two months together, was it that our differences had become more apparent, were our interests taking us on diverging tracks ... ? We were both off to university only six weeks later and I really cannot remember what happened in that period.

I can, however, vividly remember arriving at Sheffield University in Freshers Week and being bowled over by the realisation of the enormous change that was about to happen to my life. I would be living in a city for the first time, starting up a demanding degree course at a northern university far from home and with wine, women, song and the freedom of the 60's open to me. I loved my course, the new people I met, being treated as an adult, getting into an intense relationship with a woman for the first time and so forth. Although I still did a few of the old things – I rowed for the University and played rugby for the Faculty of Architecture – my priorities and interests changed.

It was a hard slog to succeed in getting through five unbroken years at Sheffield, in order to receive my degree in 1969. My girlfriend was a teacher at a school for children with learning disabilities as well as, for many, physical disabilities. I spent a fair bit of time at the school and the need to care for all people, that my parents had drilled into me, was reinforced. My final year's thesis project was a specialist hospital centre for assessing, recommending placements and teaching children with multiple disabilities. I took the decision on graduation to try to work on projects particularly associated with the physical, mental, educational and social wellbeing of people. What follows is how I pursued my intention by choosing where to work and why, and on what main projects I was involved.

Following guidelines for first post-graduation architectural jobs, I worked at ADP[1] in Henley-on-Thames, Oxfordshire for

1 ADP – Architects Design Partnership, by coincidence architects to our art teacher Robin Pitman for his house.

just two years, it being near to where my parents then lived and where there was lots of rowing going on. I worked on housing for elderly and disabled people and a hospital out-patient department, while spending evening and weekends rowing in Henley Rowing Club's 1st eight. I learnt a lot – thanks to caring colleagues and by often working through the night because I felt I was too slow in moving projects along – and reached the point where I was able to take final exams to register as an architect. I decided to go to London, hanging up my oar for the time being.

My first London job, starting in '71, was at DRU[2] where I went at the behest of Kenneth Bayes[3], whom I knew from being the partner of a student who had studied with me and who had suggested the subject for my final year's thesis project outlined above. Through Ken, DRU was working with the UK Department of Health (DOH) to establish guidelines and architectural solutions to move people from the old "Mental Institutions" to community-based care. I gained experience working on a range of projects:

- housing for the elderly and people with disabilities
- housing with adjacent training centres for adults with learning difficulties
- housing with adjacent schools for children with learning difficulties
- turned my university thesis into reality (same city, different site)
- master planning for town centre reorganisations to make them accessible by people with disabilities
- Hong Kong Mass Transit railway

While at DRU and with their encouragement I applied for and was awarded a Winston Churchill Fellowship, which took me to most Scandinavian countries to study their health and housing structures for the proper integration of "minority" groups of the population into society, including people with all types of physical and/or mental disabilities. These were much further developed than anything in the UK at that time. On my return, I attended several International Architectural

2    DRU – Design Research Unit, founded by Marcus Brumwell, Misha Black and Milner Gray in 1943. One of the first generation of British design consultancies combining expertise in architectural, graphic and industrial design. Known in its early days for its role in the 1951 Festival of Britain and many corporate identities including British Rail.

3    Kenneth Bayes – Partner/Director at DRU from 1945. As well as designing many buildings he wrote papers and books about the design of buildings for people with learning disabilities taking Rudolf Steiner's philosophy around the "biography of architecture" as the foundation.

Psychology Conferences[4] and gave a paper at the one in Belgium.

By '76 I had, however, become anxious to improve my skills in running large projects and dealing with national and international contractors. Paul James, ex-DOH hospital guru, involved in developing Best Buy, Harness and Nucleus (all fast-tracking design systems for large general hospitals), had set up HDP[5] after leaving DOH and was looking for somebody to take some of the load off him and perhaps replace him later – I got the job. One project very important to me was the upgrading and extension of Westminster Hospital, London, the hospital in which I was born. Others included:
- Design proposals for bespoke health developments in UK and overseas
- Private hospitals
- Surgical blocks in London

In my time at HDP, I gained a lot of experience, confidence, and the ability to handle large projects and contracting organisations, but I needed to get back to a closer link to people, so in '81 I decided to move on.

I joined S&W[6] who needed somebody like me with hospital and large project experience to help them with a private hospital in Scotland. I celebrated a much-needed return to high quality architectural design and the wellbeing of people:
- full design proposals for a private hospital in Glasgow
- housing refurbishment for east London housing association involving in-depth community consultation
- diagnostic and surgical hospital for the RAF to receive service personnel repatriated from theatres of war

4      International Architectural Psychology Conferences – Conferences to promote the scientific debate over the most recent empirical findings and theoretical advances in environmental psychological science, and to stimulate peer-to-peer discussions in qualified networks on the relationship between humans and their environment.

5      HDP – Hospital Design Partnership was a specialist company that designed hospitals and related health buildings in the UK, Africa, Middle East, and Far East for both national and private health providers.

6      S&W – Spence and Webster, founded by Robin Spence, when he won the international architectural competition for the New Parliamentary Building in Westminster in 1971 with Robin Webster. Their design was in fact quietly dropped by the government in 1976, and much later Portcullis House designed by Hopkins was built. The practice was greatly influenced by the work of Mies van der Rohe.

In '84 I joined ACP[7] for what was going to be a demanding but very rewarding 10yrs. Their health team was under increasing pressure, and they needed somebody with my background to spread the load. ACP was only the third company in the UK to start using computer aided drawing, opening up a much bigger market to serve using digital information transfer. During my time there, I worked on:
- general hospital and many related health projects in the west of England
- 600-bed private hospital in Hong Kong (HK)
- a series of upgrades and expansions for Nuffield Hospitals throughout the UK
- re-siting of UK's military hospital in HK prior to the end of the UK's lease of HK

One of my most important and demanding projects at ACP took me back to my very early life when on the radio there was always talk of a thing or place called 'garser' – which I later understood was actually Gaza – a 250 bed general hospital for the UN in the Gaza Strip. This was desperately needed for the care of Palestinians living in what was then the 2nd most densely populated part of our planet. It had to be designed and tendered within one year including briefing and consultation with medics in Gaza as well as the UN. The demands of this project greatly helped me to get through a very difficult phase of my personal life.

Newly re-married, in '94 I joined my best man at my first marriage in his practice, called Sprunt, for my last 15 years of working formally as an architect. Rob Sprunt had worked for me as a student at DRU and had been in public offices since completing his training and before forming Sprunt. The practice's work on local authority housing and education projects was growing rapidly, such that Rob needed somebody with the big project experience I had. My having had experience in the health field for some time soon attracted health projects.
- extensive refurbishment of whole east London housing estates, including making them have better and more accessible accommodation for people with disabilities

---

7    ACP – Architects Co-Partnership, set up in 1939 by a group of recent graduates of the Architectural Association School of Architecture wanting a new sort of practice in which hierarchy would be abolished and all members would be equal. The Architects Co-Operative Partnership, as it was originally called, was committed in equal measure to the social programme and the aesthetic renewal of modern architecture. One of their early projects was the Brynmawr Rubber factory in Wales.

- primary care centres that brought individual small GP practices together under one roof to share up-to-the-moment health facilities
- more primary care centres from Sprunt winning one of the Private Finance Initiative NHS Lift projects in London
- acute care hospital in Bangalore, India
- large high-tech dental hospital for Kuwait
- several education projects in London

Towards the end of my time at Sprunt I advised local authorities on how to resolve contractual difficulties on housing and education projects as well as getting Sprunt Quality Management accreditation.

Well, how do you think I did against the decision taken at my graduation 40 years earlier to concentrate on projects particularly associated with the physical, mental, educational, and social wellbeing of people?

*\*\*\**

The only firm memory I have of meeting Leon post Trip64 is a lunch with him and his wife at their flat in Primrose Hill, London in the early 70's. Since then, there was no contact, until well after my retirement when I started to think about friends from my youth (as you do when you're heading into your dotage), and I found an email address for Leon. I wrote on 11 May 17:

> Hello Leon,
>
> Do you remember Borlase School, rowing on the Thames, Robin Pitman, sketching in a pub in Cookham, cycling to Rome in 1964? Well so do I.
> Yes, it's that John Turner person, who now lives in France with his lovely wife Annie.
> With the Tour de France coming up soon I thought, today, that old cycling friends might like to make contact.
> If you would like to share the last 40yrs-ish of fun in this world, since we last met, please get back to me.
>
> Regards,
> John

To which Leon replied immediately:

```
            Dear John,

    I remember it very well indeed!
            Your email reached me in the lounge at Dubai as
    I return home after my spring visit to Europe. Back
    late autumn.
            A lifetime since we met.
            Roger Sandilands made contact last year...
            I've seen Peter Flowerday in the past year...

            Goodness!
            Leon
```

After keeping in touch from time to time, early in autumn 2020 Leon floated the idea of producing a book about our 1964 cycle ride to Rome, based on the writings, photographs, drawings, etc. that we produced through the trip. By the late autumn we were underway, searching for potential data from the days before computers. I spent a lot of time on collating and cataloguing what was found and Leon on working out the timeline of the trip and transcribing his handwritten daily journal. There were a few tense moments working together building the Trip64 story, but we have now come out the other side and our original friendship has shone through after more than half a century!

* * *

From when I was a toddler and able to hold a crayon, pencil or pen I enjoyed drawing. From the early days the only thing I actually remember drawing were hills, one behind another, not surprising living as I did then in the Chiltern Hills above Marlow, Buckinghamshire. I took to making my own birthday cards for family and friends, which soon developed into the mass production of most of my family's Christmas cards.

    As soon as I started infant school, I developed a squint and when I was 7 had an operation to correct it. Post-op, I had to do "bar-reading" every day to make both eyes work together. We visited Maidenhead hospital where an orthoptist, Miss Todd, checked how I was doing by sitting close to me face to face as I put images of lions and the like into cages, using handles on a mechanical device before the days of computers. I fell in love with her, but nothing developed. This enforced activity, Miss Todd excluded, put me off reading for life but increased my drawing activities. Looking back, it is surprising I got through school and even more, university.

When I started at Borlase School, Marlow in 1957, I was thus well prepared to benefit from our art teacher Robin Pitman's excellent teaching, to which we have both referred. I was proud of my artistic abilities in some areas, but when Leon joined the school, I realised my talents were way behind. Because of the enforced "bar reading" my literary prowess was way behind my drawing but, as part of preparing for the A-level examination that I had to do in half the normal time, a fair bit of reading was a must. One book I read was E. H. Gombrich's "The Story of Art", first published 1950 (I still have my tenth edition of 1960). I remember amazing my mother by saying "I'm really enjoying reading this book", something she had never heard before – my interests in the visual arts had perhaps unlocked the literary side of my brain! When we decided to embark on Trip64, I thought there could be an opportunity for some private tuition from Leon. This started with beer drinking and sketching in a pub called the Bel & The Dragon in Cookham near where he lived and thankfully continued during our journey to Rome.

As I was collating and cataloguing my drawings on to a spreadsheet, I included a "rating" column. Each drawing was given a rating by me of Very Poor, Poor, OK, Good or Very Good (VP, P, OK, G or VG), mainly for Leon's benefit since he had not seen any of the drawings since Trip64. Holland and Germany collected "nil points", i.e.no G's or VG's, but:
- Austria notched up 18% of its drawings with a G;
- Northern Italy 27% G and 24% VG and
- Rome 32% G and 58% VG!

Was there the improvement in my drawing abilities by the time I reached Rome that I had hoped for? Clearly, I believe now there was – what do you think? I built on what I had learnt on Trip64 through the 5 year's study for a degree in architecture and then used it during my 40 formal years practicing the art of architecture for the benefit, I hope, of peoples' lives.

### Before Trip64

Unfortunately, the only examples of my work prior to Trip64, to which I currently have access, are two pieces of sculpture. Here I was exploring how basically 2 dimensional pieces of wood could be modelled to bring the 3rd dimension alive and, in the case of the fish, to hint at the 4th dimension.

## Holland

I was disappointed and surprised, when I finally unearthed my Trip64 drawings, that I had done very few before we reached Munich and only two before I met up with Leon in Amsterdam. At Borlase, I had done few drawings of buildings, so it was not surprising when I tried this in Delft (Day 25) that I had a lot to learn. A nervous start with my new Flowmaster pen on the first drawing, then adding a normal pen to look at shadows cast on a façade in the second – later at university I learnt this to be the gentle art of skiagraphy. I thought, I mused, I had a way to go, but had the relief that my private tutor, Leon, would be around soon.

## Travelling from the Rhine to arrival in Munich

After our ride south out of Holland, up the Rhine and then east towards Munich, we arrived in the medieval town of Schwäbisch Hall. Not until Day 38 did my pens touch paper again, but they had to come out then for Schwäbisch Hall. With some care and understanding, Leon led me forward on how to relax, look at buildings as they really are and record this on a piece of paper. I was delighted and relieved by these early results.

## Munich

The Hofbräuhaus in Munich took me back to the sketching sessions of people in Cookham, but I decided to try out a slightly new approach to drawing with my new pens. However, there were also many classical buildings to be seen in this major city in the south of Germany. The beer was not the same in the Hofbräuhaus as that in Cookham, but the scope for sketching was vastly better. I believe these drawings were done on Day 43, the day of our apparent second "temper tantrum". I did quite a few that session in the Hofbräuhaus and the ones shown here may have been a couple of the later ones after more than a few beers. I then drew my first classical style building on Trip64 – the dome of Justizpalast (a court building) – and again realised I still had a long way to go in my quest for good quality drawing skills.

## Travelling from Munich and time in Salzburg

After Munich, we headed to Salzburg for a stay of almost a week with some of Leon's relatives. It was here that I started to think my drawing might be turning the corner. On Day 45, I drew the horse fountain in Residenzplatz, which I was pleased turned out to be delicate and calm, as well as like a real fountain. On Day 47, we spent a good part of the day in the relatives' house, and I slowly and meticulously drew the row of houses behind. Very boring drawing, but I believe it to be

accurate. Then, on Day 48, the pièce de résistance north of the Alps — I drew a back street downtown somewhere, that I felt hit most of the buttons if I wanted to say I could draw quite well. Not a lot of drawing went on while in Salzburg, so these three perhaps pivotal drawings can be seen in the main pages of the Journal.

## Venice

Over the Alps by train for a stay of almost a week again, this time in Venice. What I thought was my almost daily improvement in drawing abilities levelled out now, compared with those necessary improvements north of the Alps. The afternoon following our arrival in Venice on Day 53, I drew the entrance and domed roofscape of St Marks, only my second drawing after little sleep on the train from Salzburg. Not bad I thought. On return home I painted a gouache version of this as a thank you to my parents for their help with Trip64, but unfortunately it was on a previously used old piece of hardboard, as can be seen.

The next day lots of drawing was done and I particularly liked one of those I did of Santa Maria della Salute. Both these drawings were very much a step on from my first attempts in Munich to draw a large public building.

My last drawing in Venice was done on a day we walked about a lot and saw many minor streets. One is looking down such a street. Again, a much better attempt than those in Schwäbisch Hall and maybe a fraction better than the one in Salzburg. I think I was still making improvements.

### Travelling from Venice and time in Florence

As we pressed on, I found I was looking more at spaces between buildings, upper parts of buildings and roof landscapes, something that has stuck with me ever since. I find more visual interest here than in formal street level facades. An example of this development is my drawing of some vernacular buildings – with a formal structure peeping over the top – drawn from the edge of Vicenza.

This trend developed further, by adding the integration of vernacular and formal structures, street level activity and things overhead to the mix, as I looked down one of the streets by San Lorenzo in Florence and also in street scenes drawn elsewhere in Florence.

Giotti's campanile ↓

Florence
64

In the Journal, I made my feelings about Florence clear when we arrived on the evening of Day 64 – *"Florence was my most loved place visited on Trip64"*. Primarily, this love sprang from the pleasure given to me by the relaxed and intimate relationship between the grand public buildings and the surrounding normal vernacular buildings. I prepared an essay on Florence during the production of this book and an extract follows:

"On our second day as we left the cloisters in the Laurentian Library, the view of tiled roofs with the Duomo and the Campanile beyond did capture the contrast between the formal and the basic buildings I loved so much in Florence.

I had always enjoyed walking through densely packed streets and then entering a large single volume such as the combination of a nave, transept and chancel of an English church or cathedral. In these cases, it's the spatial jolt combined with the change in illumination level that gives me the buzz. Even today in our local seaside town, Les Sables d'Olonne, in France, I get this buzz when entering the main church, but Florence Cathedral did a lot more. The sensory changes themselves are one thing, but it also gets one thinking back to what went on there - in Les Sables the mariners and fishermen who would have been laid to rest and in Florence the highs, lows and trauma of the early Renaissance.

Back to the outside, to my beloved juxta-positioning of massive formal buildings, crammed into a simple domestic street. In 1964, the amount of traffic on narrow roads and the overhead tram lines added to the drama. I started by sketching small features of the formal buildings to try to understand their structure and design. Later, I confronted the big boys and the streetscapes around them.

The three separate elements of the cathedral, Duomo, Baptistry and Campanile sank home for the first time and prepared me for Pisa. The logic and reality of the three elements is obvious when one thinks about it. Each element can be used independently and at the same time, unlike the cathedrals we know in England.

The three elements also had the effect of pulling in the external spaces around to be part of the whole. The physically simple, homogeneous nature of the cathedral group - compared with the more defined identification of the separate elements of an English cathedral, where the nave, the aisles, the transept and the chancel are expressed very distinctly in plan and section, but within a single building - was new to

FIG. 32.

Maggiore
Rome—64

me, as was the visually powerful marble cladding of the external face of the buildings.

Both within the city and from all around, the cathedral and its related buildings are seldom out of sight. During our stay in Florence the cathedral area became our most visited "old friend".

## Rome

Arriving in Rome directed me back to concentrating on the enormous number of formal classical buildings. My drawings of Santa Maria Maggiore and Sant 'Andrea della Valle both show, in my mind, better drawing ability and confidence than any of my earlier drawings of similar buildings.

Well, was there an improvement in my drawing abilities between Holland and Rome?

\* \* \*

I will never forget Trip64 and am so pleased Leon and I decided to work together to interface our memories and writings, drawings, photos, and various artifacts that have survived since 1964. In 1964 Italy was so different from England. Despite WW2 having moved up from its toes to its junction with the Alps, there was fun and colour all around and although many people were very poor, it did not seem to matter. The destruction of important works of art, including buildings, was surprisingly limited by comparison with parts of London and in many industrial cities around England, where bombing had been intense.

It was a pleasure to be in Italy in the early 60's.

Vicenza: Several subjects: (top left) Street scene; (top right) Idealised female figure in arcade; (middle) View of Villa Rotonda from the road; (bottom left) Villa Rotonda from inside the boundary wall and (bottom left) John cycling with paniers to the fore. The seeming perfect symmetry of the villa has haunted architects, but Andrew Hopkins has proved the symmetry to be an illusion.

In mid-September 2021 John and I agreed final versions of three transcripts. One covered my time in Belgium and Holland, one covered our journey from our meeting up in Amsterdam, the cycling to Salzburg, and our time there until we embarked on a train to Venice; the third from Venice to Rome and back home. The hand-written journals were back in storage, with a transcript of the second typed in duplicate by my mother in the 1960s. Part of the fair copy is missing – this had been sent to London to my father's cousin Tjaart Coetsee, then a writer in the Africa service of the BBC. 'Florid and immature' sums up his discouraging response. He might have mentioned the journals of Patrick Leigh Fermor, which inevitably come to mind, and with which no comparison could or can survive. Why then have I persisted? In part to discover whether I now think that Tjaart's assessment was valid. (I don't!) In part because we have captured a moment of innocence in a Europe still recovering from WW2, in part because while we did not have access to the grand houses of pre-war aristocracies, we were buffeted by the actualities of a time, pre the Beeching cuts to the British rail network, outlined in two reports, one in 1963, the second in 1965. The roads were not yet dominated by cars, to an extent difficult now to imagine. I wrote to John expressing this in elaboration of a statement in my journal:

"'A time without cars' had a contemporary aspect to it. Cycling through rural Holland, I seldom encountered a car. The context for this may be illustrated by the fact that in 1960 there were about 5 million cars registered in the UK, whereas in 2020 there were almost 32 million. I recall a day cycling along a road traversing the base of a dyke, lushly pastured polder meadows on my right, long grass waves rippling along the dyke to my left. A gloriously sunny and fresh early spring day. Eventually propelled by curiosity I lay my bike on the grass and climbed to the top of the dyke. There I surprised a few courting couples, lying looking out across the cold grey sea. It was only in Italy that we felt the press of cars and lorries; literally by John, who was grazed by a lorry as we cycled up (as I recall it), down (as he remembers it) the Apennines."

Mostly we agree about the facts of the joint journey, until we reach Rome that is. Then there are huge discrepancies in our recollections. We cannot pin down the date that we left. I know that I went to the Swiss National Exposition in Lausanne, and I have total recall of the architecture of the show – an ingenious canvas tectonic that has been a major influence on me over the years. Yet John has no recollection of this. I vividly remember us laughing at our bloated or elongated reflections in the distorting mirrors that were the final event of the show. Maybe this presaged Carlo Rovelli's statement in Helgoland (Allen Lane 2021, p165), which I am reading as we work our way to a conclusion of this account of our trip: Reality has broken into a play of mirrors. I find that remembering is like entering a hall of distorting mirrors. While grappling with this dissonance in our recollections, I came across an anecdote in the book 'In Memory of Memory' by Maria Stepanova, translated by Susan Dugdale, (Fitzcarraldo Editions, 2021, pp 53–54). In my words: Stepanova makes a long journey to the town her great, great, grandfather came from. The house he lived in had been identified from the census by a local academic. She spends the afternoon imagining and 'remembering' how the family lived in this courtyard house. She leaves convinced that she has embedded within herself an authentic memory, down to the Rudbeckias along the base of a wall. A day later the academic sheepishly tells her on the phone that he identified the wrong house. "That street all right, but a different house." She concludes "And that is just about everything I know about memory."

Back to "An age without cars." This – in the transcription – refers to my grandfather's childhood in Zierekzee, where – in family legend – his father, a cabinet maker, would not let his children wear shoes because if people saw them well-shod, they would not pay their bills. And I wrote in anticipation of my visit to the town: "... better be good to have kept its young. Well, it didn't..." As its web states, the tiny city was a wealthy trading port in the Middle Ages, and 'its wealth led to the construction of a beautiful port, city hall, mills, church and city walls and gates...' My great, great grandfather, the kapellmeister at the main church, the Nieuwe Kerk, choirmaster and arranger of music, was buoyed up on the tail-end of the glory days. By my great grandfather's time Zierikzee was resting on past glories. So 'better be good' – it once was, and this accounts for my family's migration down the Rhine from Schaikseheide (Schaik's Heath) near Nijmegen or Schaiksedijk Schaik's Dike) near Eindhoven. But by my grandfather's generation the city was locked into an economic (and according to his younger sister, my great aunt Greta in Amsterdam) a cultural stasis, nowadays relieved only by tourism. At the age of 21, Oupa accompanied his two older brothers when they left to set up a printing press (still operating) for the Boer Republic of the Transvaal. The daily passing of tourists through Zierikzee no doubt caused the ennui of the postcard shop lady, who was less than interested in my origin story. Why, I wonder, did I spend so little time there? My visit was a cursory ticking of a box, rather than an archaeological delving. I was, I think, both curious about the past and impatient for the future. More interested in Dutchness than in finding the actual houses of the kapellmeister and the cabinet maker. A decade later my Aunt Betty arrived in London with a street map identifying those houses and she set off to visit the actual sites.

There is a degree of memory excavation or memory creation going on here. Uneasy with this – as I think all memoirists are – I searched for more abstract ways of interrogating what we recorded and thought about the photos that we took. I made screen shots of the photos that I find charismatic and considered in the manner of Susan Sontag what the framing of the content revealed. Pointing a camera has a history of causing a compulsion to composition that radically edits or crops what is seen, and under the influence of our art master at Borlase, we were no exception to this! I believe that there is a consistent compositional attitude to what makes a picture, to what is important to us in architecture and landscape that reveals a shared aesthetic, forged in the art studio at school. It is very much of its time, pared back, pretty. Then I wondered about details in the photos that 'pop' the text into focus, things like the big American car on the bank of a canal in Delft, a Beehive hairdo and Chanel suit in Munich, our laden bicycles in Italy ... There was a 'pop' sensibility in the air, we were primed in this framing by our recent exposure to works in the Whitechapel Gallery in London, very much in contradiction to the arts and craft sensibility that permeated our art master's world

As I am sure Susan Sontag[1] observed, long after we made our trip, pointing a camera is a complex and revealing act. The photo tells you a great deal about the mental space that guided the pointing. For those brought up in England (and in the anglosphere), the history of looking at landscape and buildings is tied up with the Grand Tours of the 17th, 18th and 19th centuries. As Christopher Hussey[2] points out in his book on the Picturesque, a book that I read in 1967, until this time landscapes that were admired were productive rather than 'sublime'. The landscape painters changed the perceptions of the educated elites, and travellers carried gilded frames with a handle to assist them in framing up digestible images of what they were seeing from their carriages. Claude mirrors, "Gray glasses", named after landscape painter Claude Lorraine

---

1  Sontag, Susan, 1979, On Photography, Penguin, London
2  Hussey, Christopher, 1967, The Picturesque, Studies in Point of View, Frank Cass & Co. Ltd., London

(1600–1682) or the poet Thomas Gray (1716–1771), were all the rage for a time. Travellers would turn their backs on vistas and look at them in these hand-held mirrors, clouded to give a 'soft mellow tinge' as in a painting.

In my own slides and I believe in John's, I can discern a balancing of elements so that for example, a highlight is located towards the middle of the picture, with flanking material becoming secondary or subsumed in a chiaroscuro dramatization of light bracketed by shadow. Or the picture plane is split into three vertical zones with a building of detail to a climax in one or other of the peripheral thirds.

Was there an alternative? Certainly Ed Ruscha (1937–) engaged in a very different kind of photography. A "dirty realism" approach that defied picturesque aesthetics. "Twenty Six Gasoline Stations" (1963) betrays his awareness of composition because the photos betray the same partis that we were unconsciously in thrall to; but "Every Building on the Sunset Strip" (1966) consisting of photos of every building on both sides of the 24 miles of Hollywood Boulevard eschews that history for an attempt at realism. This artist's book and his "Thirty Four Parking Lots in Los Angeles" (1967), a set of aerial views of car parks that reveals the patterns of use by recording the oil leaks from cars – both in my personal library since 1968 – embark on a new way of looking through the camera which we were innocent of in 1964.

Few, if any of our photos are 'realist' in this sense. All of them can be enhanced by a slight reframing, a fact which to my mind proves that there was composing going on. We were yet not attuned to the ideas about dirty realism and new beauty that were already being pursued in the avant-garde, but soon I had abandoned my conservative career plans in favour of the experimentation going on at Newcastle upon Tyne under the auspices of artist Richard Hamilton, the acknowledged coiner of the term 'Pop Art'. In part my change of direction was prompted by the call of the sexual fluidity that characterised the decade, a fluidity on display at Newcastle when I went for an interview, and a fluidity expressly disparaged by our art master who was very much into a bohemianism of wine women and song – and as on one occasion – cheese! He returned from a holiday in France with a car laden with cheese which he realised was all about to go off, so everyone he knew including his sixth formers were invited to consume them, which we did one wine-fuelled evening.

I come to a startling trick of memory that emerged as we worked through the transcription. As the journal reaches the Apennines, I recall peeling off the road and walking directly into an 'osteria'. Checking the timeline itinerary, I find the osteria on the right-hand side of the road. My recollection is all about peeling to the left. There is an osteria to the left, one building back from the road. We could not have 'peeled off' to it. Then I realise that all along I have read my journal as if I, and then we, were cycling on the left-hand side of the road. Which of course we never were. So, my memory has reorganised itself into a left-hand drive model, an interesting falsity!

What is missing? Frances Wilson writes this in 'Burning Man' her 2021 biography of D H Lawrence:

p273 "The reader of a good travel book is entitled not only to an exterior voyage, to a description of scenery and so forth, but to an interior, a sentimental or temperamental voyage, which takes place side by side with the outer one." (Norman Douglas, review of Charles Montagu Doughty's Travels in Arabia Deserta)

We are silent about our desires, except for noting the beauty of many of the young women we encountered. Maybe after all we were way too young to express our feelings, very much hemmed in by the expectations of our elders. Indeed, by the expectations of each other!

We were subject to forces larger than our individual lives and now, 57 years later, it is evident that the dynamics that pushed Europe and Asia into the devastating conflicts of WW2 are still at work. In the face of this ever-threatening external world, I can only pursue what, in his late film Fanny and Alexander (1982), Ingmar Bergman termed 'the little life of family and friends', of gardening and of living in what seems to be a responsible way. "The world is a den of thieves" says the actor playing Fanny and Alexander's uncle, "and night is closing in. So come let us celebrate." And he raises his glass to toast the extended family assembled around the table.

In his 2021 book Albert and the Whale, (4th Estate) Philip Hoare notes on page 177: "There were three acts to your life, (Auden) knew from Kierkegaard. The first was the passing moment of sensation; the second, involvement and responsibility; the third, understanding that there is no inheritance and no matter what you do, good may not result. You could only abandon yourself to despair, or throw yourself on the mercy of God."

This rings true to me as I garden into the southern spring of 2021. Our second acts were indeed full of involvement and responsibilities; as to our third acts, we speak a little in these reflections. Apropos the quotation above, I take God to be Physics! As Carlo Rovelli writes in Helgoland (Allen Lane 2021, p69): Quantum theory is the theory of how things influence each other. And this connective entanglement is often at a great distance, as it has been in John's and my case. The early sensate wonder of our trip has permeated our lives.

So – considering the internalities of our first acts, this book captures us at a cusp moment between our teens and our adult lives. I commend the immediacy of the words of the journal and of our drawings and photographs. These were written, drawn, and snapped at the time. They capture our wonder, and they speak for themselves.

Angier, Carole, *Speak, Silence: In Search of W. G. Sebald*, Bloomsbury, 2021, London
Antonioni, Michelangelo, *The Red Desert*, 1964, Ravenna
Baudrillard, Jean, *The Consumer Society*, Sage Publications, 1970
Cole, Lance, CITROEN DS, Pen and Sword Books, 2021, Barnsley
Evelyn, John (1620-1706), The Diary of John Evelyn (31 October 1620-27 February 1706), first published 1818 with a second edition in 1819 under the title *Memoirs Illustrative of the Life and Writings of John Evelyn*, edited by William Bray.
Fabes, Stephen, *Signs of Life, To the Ends of the Earth with a Doctor*, Profile Books, 2020, London. A doctor cycles around the world for a year.
Fellini, Federico, *Juliet of The Spirits*, 1965, Fregene, Rome
Fermor, Patrick Leigh, *Between the Woods and the Water*, Penguin, 1986/7, London
Flora, Peter, *Growth to Limits: The Western European Welfare State Since World War II*, 1986.
Forrester, David, *Post-war Europe*, London Review of Books, Vol 34, No.1, 31 Jan, 2021.
Frommer, Arthur, *Europe on 5 Dollars a Day*, 1957
Gombrich E. H. *The Story of Art*, 1950, 1960
Hopkins, Andrew, *Neither Perfect, Nor Ideal: Palladio's Villa Rotonda*, in SAHGB (journal of society of architectural historians, GB), 2022
Gunn, Thom, *Rapallo*, in *Boss Cupid*, Faber and Faber, 1992
Pitman, Robin, *Robin Pitman Art Master*, introduced by Hugh Wheldon, BBC Monitor, Wed 12 August 1964, directed by Nancy Thomas.
Marais, Eugene, The Soul of the White Ant, 1937, first published in Afrikaans in 1925, p83
Pevsner, Nicholas and Williamson, Mary, *The buildings of England: Buckinghamshire*, Penguin Books, 1960, London
Robson, Graham, *AZ British Cars 1945-1980*, Herridge and Sons, 2006, UK
Rovelli, Carlo, Helgoland, Allen Lane, 2021, London
YHA, *YHA History*, <yha.org.uk>

Map outline by Orion 8 https://commons.wikimedia.org/w/index.php?curid=7381947

INDEX

This index authored by Leon is inspired by the book *Index, A History of* (see Bibliography), in which this quote from Wordsworth's *The Prelude, or Growth of a Poet's Mind* (1850) does not have a place:
> "The marble index of a mind forever / Voyaging through strange seas of Thought, alone." The real index lies in what we saw, apt for two budding architects. This gives a taste of that.

A

Architects: Alvar Aalto p27, Asam p165, Berlage, H. P. architect of Gemeente Museum, The Hague, p 79, Breuer, Marcel De Bijenkorf p73 Euromast p73, Van Den Broek and Bakema, De Lijnbaan p71, p107, Brinkman and van der Vlught, Van Nelle Factory 1925-1931, p77 Palladio p223, Villa Rotonda p225, Ponti, Gio p227, Brunelleschi p257, Michelangelo p259, p327, Elia Volpi p269, Michelozzi p277, Giotto p279, Bernini p297, Borrimini p297, Nervi p329, Design Research Unit (DRU) p342, Spence and Webster p343, Architects Co-Partnership (ACP) p344, Sprunt p344

Artists: Brinker, Hans, statue of small boy with finger in small dyke, at Spaarndam p89, Calder, Alexander p93, Constant, *New Babylon* p81 Cornelis van Haarlem, struck by p87, Devriendt, Lucas, *Paint it black, my research into the Black Plastic as a self-portrait in the Cabinet Devriendt* p81, Hals, Frans, makes me laugh p87, Hamilton, Richard, *The Sainsbury Wing 1999-2000*, twinned with Saenradem by use of black square on the diagonal p81, p219, p366, Klee, Paul p161 Kokoschka p181, Lucebert, member of COBRA p81, Maes, Nicholas, *Het Gebed* ca 1656 p93, Mondrian, Piet p75, Paul Klee idem, influences on p81, Moore, Henry p73, idem p95, p166, p181, Naum Gabo, Zadkine, Ossip, Belarus born French artist p73, Nevelson, Louise p93, Noguchi, p93, Picasso, Guernica, p73, Picasso, *Aubergine*, p93, Rembrandt, Nightwatch p101, Rodin p95, Saura, Antonio, Spanish artist and writer p93, Sluyters, Jan, post-impressionist p87, Tapies I Puig, Antoni, 1923-2012, 1st Marquess of Tapies, Barcelona based sculptor and painter P 53, Toorop, Jan, impressed p81, Vermeer, Jan, *View of Delft 1660-61*, enjoyed p81, Wagemaker, Jaap, Dutch painter p115, Lorenzo Veneziano p213, Jacoba del Fiore p213, Nicolo de Pietro p213, Giovani Bellini p213, Giorgione p213, p263, Ghiberti p253, p263, p273, Pisano p253, Donatello p253, p273, Giotto p253, p277, Michelangelo p253, p255, Cellini p255, Vasari p257, Valerio Cioli p267, Della Robbia p271, Gambognola p273, Massacio p273, p277, Lippi p277, Giovani Pisano p283, Nicholas Pisano p283, Bernini p327, p331

Art Biennale di Venezia No. 32: Caballero, p217, Gentils P217, Bury p217, Arpel p219, Passmore p219, Caprogessi p219, Tapies p219, Calder p219, Cezar p219, Giacometti p219, Cagli p219, Savelli p219, Cavaliere p219, Mari p219, Rauschenberg p219, p221, Johns p219, p221, Nolan p219, Louis p219, Hilton p219, Tilson p219, Duchamp p219

Art movements: Fauve p161, Blaue Reiter p161, COBRA p81, Vormentaal p81, Cretan School p217, Gruppe Enne Padova p219

Artefacts: Murano glass, Wedgwood p101

## B

Beer: long for a p47, Stella Artois p51, Heineken beer p91, brewery p123, in pottery mugs p131, cool beer, cheese and mustard, p123, p125, outside in the shade p145, Hofbrauhaus p163

Borlase, Sir William's School: p6, p15, p17, p21, p23, p25, p37, p41, p71

Breakfast: Gouda Cheese p93, Netherlandish, enormous p109, Ersatzkaffee p133, vollkornbrot and treacle p155, toasted rolls p177, seven peaches and half a litre of milk p227, vino dolce and rolls p231, Nutella and bread p247, coffee, milk and sweet rolls p289

Buildings: see timelines for locales, passim

## C

Cities and towns: see timelines for locales and p27, p43, p47, p51, p58, p73, p113, p117, p123, p137, p159, p167, p173, p197, p207, p209, p217, p225, p239, p253, p259, p263, p267, p271, p279, p281, p295, p265, p335, p341, p343, p349, p361, p364

## D

Drinks, hot: Chocolate, endless pots of tea, p69, tea, literally p79, chocolate p161, Rooibos p171, farewell p191, morning coffee p225, tea in a hot bar p295

Drinks, soft: Lemonade, drinking while watching Moores and Rodins p95, Coca Cola, Trink p143, in Gasthof lounge p147, a litre of water and p149, a coke p155, Si-Si lemonade idem, Coca Cola p203, enough, not eating p145, bloated p175, espressos p243, p265, Pepsi Colas p283, water and cola p289, aqua p289

G

Galleries and museums: Stadhuis, Gouda 1415, Yellowstone, red and white triangles p77, Gemeente Museum, The Hague p81, Mauritiushuis 'leaves me cold' p81, Rijks Museum p93, Stedelijk Museum, p91, p115, p123, Jewish Museum, Amsterdam, the German occupation, horror of p97, Ons Liewe Heer op Solder, concealed catholic church p97, Rembrandt's House, etchings and drawings, interior with winding stair enthrals, p101, Willet Holthuysen House p101, Stadtische p161, Scuolo Grande di San Rocco p211, Gallerie Accademia p213, Museum of Byzantium p217, 32nd Biennale di Venice p217-219, USA annexe p221, Uffizi p263, Palazzo Pitti p267, Palazzo Davanzati p269, Medici Palace p273, Bargello p273, Swiss national Exposition p333

Gardens: p41, p55, p59, p52, p63, p169, p175, p239, p249, p295, p367

Girls: Leon's Australians p10, daughter, "You are not sleeping with my …!" p 67, how cycle in a tight skirt p79, from Berlin p81 from Munster, liked p85 Australian, Leon bought beer for, p91, fab group of p139, fab directs p161, an even better idem, soft arms p221, in black bulges p241, passing p253, nasal American p275, to impress p285, from Ohio, supports Goldwater p291

Groups: friendly p167, of boys p199, couple drinking chianti p273

I

Interiors: Art Nouveau living room p81, Breuer, Marcel, chair and other Bauhaus furniture p81, Saenradem, Peter, *Interior of the GroteKerk at Haarlem 1636-37*, twinned, p81, Peter de Hooch interiors remind me of Mondriaan p93

L

Landscapes: see timelines for locales and p73, p127, p135, p217, p239, p281, p353, p365, passim

Lunch: bun and ham p41, too expensive p43, minty farm bread and carrots, p123, treacle and vollkornbrot p155, coke, vollkornbrot and sardines p161, miserable p165, on the banks of chalky river, round loaf, cheese and peanuts p167, rice, peas, mince and chives p173, spaghetti and wine p223, again p227, rolls and Nutella p231, Pizza Margherita and Vino Rossi p241, Pizza calda, frites and a peach p253, "tourist lunch' p261, spaghetti and Pastina al Brodo at Jolly Café p263, lasagne at Jolly Café p269, spaghetti and pane brood p273, spaghetti and pastina brodo again p279, chianti and pizza at Righetti p327

## M

**Men**: 'sexuale honger' p63, male form, much celebration of the p87, tough looking youngsters p123, policemen, two full length leather clad p129, prelate, red clad p129, old man, why they won the war p143, American p137, Swede p137, South Africans, three huge p143, Swimming in the Neckar p145, in smart uniforms p201, gondoliers p209, boys swimming p209, hissing p215, a caretaker p241, boys playing ball p273, chat to an American p273, Italian youths joshing p283, drivers' mates sleeping in bunks p293

**Media**: Bach p181, Beatles p205, "Mr. Heron please don't look at me..." made up song, Leon p105, "I got the hippy, hippy shake' p139, Diva, a ... shrieks p133, The Red Desert, film p239, Quando, quando p249, Imagine I'm in love with you (The Beatles) p285

## P

**Pastries**: apple p145, with strawberries and cream p155, with coffee p161, with iced coffee p161, with coffee p161, soggy p165, cherry p175, pumpernickel, biscuits, orange chocolate and milk p137, and treacle, milk and sweets p151

**People**: watching me watching them p145, couples p199, at the Lido p201, café family p203, English tourists p207, family parties p209, sleeping off the heat p211, students p217, Swedes and a couple with a baby p237, playing in the streets p241, watching p263, tourists peer p263, pour of buses p329

**Persons, named**: Harold Macmillan p7, Pitman, Robin, art master p15, p95, p281, p341, p345, p347, Sir William Borlase p21, Gwen Greene p21, Johan van Schaik p21, Percy Bysshe Shelley p23, Niklaus Pevsner p23, Great Aunt Dora p23, Dirk M p27, W.G. Sebald p27, Carole Angier p27, Geoffrey and Joan London p27, Arno, cousin of Leon p95, p113, Ernie Verlee, p83, visit to p113, Flora, Peter, and Paul Flora p71, Hill, Graham, (1929-1975) racing driver p89, Hopkins, Andrew p213, p225, John, meeting up with, who is bearded! P115, (John's) dear old dad being pot shotted at p135, Katerin is beautiful p37, Sandilands, Roger, p71 Tante Greta and Oom Karel, Leon's great aunt and great uncle p91, p123, Couzyns p169, p173, p181, p169, p245, Vittore! P259, Couzyns in Florence p263 Barry Goldwater p275, Henrich Wolflin p297, Kenneth Bayes p342, Paul James p343 Rob Sprunt p344, Miss Todd p346, p347, E. H. Gombrich p347

**Provisioning**: bread and peppermints p167, Cheese, or is it furniture polish? P151, Crayons from Ivo Haas p181, Laundromat p123, Pelikan pen p171, provisions and wine p141, sardines, cheese, soap, milk and treacle p151, bread p125, looking for milk, p253, buy peaches idem, drawing pad p259, staff at Café Jolly friendly p275, find only cheese p281, provisions p289

Punctures (Leon's): p77, p83, p87, p105, p125, p161, p167, p247, tire shreds, 'De Engelse Ding' p 135, p293, John's ball bearings lost p245, John clipped by a trailer p249

S

Snacks: at Café t"Paradijs p47, Granny Smith, p53, idem p87, SlagRoomijs (ice-cream) p81, waffle p93, Mars Bars p137, Kendal mint cake p141, Cherries, juicy local p145, sweets p169, by Suchard p185, peaches p231, gelati p239, large lump of chocolate p245, cappuccino and bread p247, coffee and lemon gelati p263, Gelati Motta disappoint p271, chocolate and orange cornetto p275, chocolate and lemon gelati p279, cola, peaches p291, tea p293, café latte, succha di frutta, tea and pizza p293, coffee, tea, such di frutta, tosti p293

Supper: soup, steak and chips, pineapple p43, enormous meal p49, meal in the hostel shack p63, at Chris's Chip Stall p65, pork, beans, potatoes, and soup p53, Food, tea and biscuits with chat p103, Leberwurst and kartoffel salad, two eggs, ham, fried toast and Bilsburger Pils p131, fine hostel meal p139, speckled sausage, rye bread, two oranges and a litre of cheap wine p143, speckled sausage, rye bread, cabbage, peanuts, cherries, apples, milk p145, at a modern hostel p147, Lowenbrau and wurst p149, in a pub: Heilbeer, tages, suppe, bratkartoffel and bratwurst p153, two eggs, soup, potato, strawberries p157, soup bread and coffee p167, pork chops, thick polenta and grilled potatoes p175, crowded in the kitchen p179, boerewors braaivleis, sausage and polenta p183, raw steak p187, bread, eggs and carrots p219, rolls, eggs, chocolate flake ice cream and wine p221, chicken p249, saltless white bread, sardines and vino p257, unsalted bread and sardines and wine p261, spaghetti and minestrone p263, bread and water p271, spaghetti, minestrone and chianti p275, lasagne, minestrone and chianti p279, bread and jam p285, bread, jam and peaches p289, four course p293, chianti and pizza at Righetti p327

T

Temper tantrum: p135, p165, p349

Theory: Central Place Theory p59, Palladio's theory p114, p225, John's university thesis p341, Leon's university thesis p342, making minestrone p265

## V

Vehicles: VandenPlas p25, American cars, p37, Peugeots, Citroens idem, Austin Van Den Plas p249, BRM, Graham Hill stalled in p89, Citroën DS p39, Citroen, aged p257, Rover P5, VandenPlas, Rover coupe, Citroen Dyane, Lancia, MG TD, Renault 4 idem, FIAT Topolino p237, Honda enthusiast p145, Rolls Royce, silver-grey at Peace Palace p81, Vauxhall Velox p173, Volkswagen Combi p65, opulent p289, lorry fumes p293, Alvis drophead coupe p295, an age without cars p364

## W

War: why won: p27, p143, after p7, p11, during p19, post p37, interwar p47, since p71, pre p115, p139, p363, memorials p123, at the end of p131, prisoner of p223, nearly won the p293, wonderful prisoner of war camps p293

Wine: Oppenheimer Kurtenbrunner 1963 p143, first Italian p219, p221, Vino Rosso p243

Women: mothers suntanning one strap at a time p95, women, painted, sunning themselves p99, nun, walking black p139, woman in polka dot dress p131, a prostitute p199, p201, flouncing with children p203, in San Marco p215, beautifully tanned p261

## ACKNOWLEDGEMENTS

John and Leon start by each recognising the efforts the other has put into preparing the materials for this reconstruction. We have perhaps devoted as much time to this as we did to the trip itself! Our very different architectural careers equally brought different skills to the overall process of creating a book of this nature.

Also, we are very grateful to John's wife Annie Jermain for keeping an eye on this process, smoothing ruffled feathers, and for boosting John's shortcomings in internet matters as well as undertaking a copy edit of the texts. Leon also appreciates the feather-smoothing efforts of his husband Andrew Keen, who has been doing this since 1965!

Posthumously we recognise what our parents contributed to the trip: John's father for supporting him in the venture despite his mother's fears; Leon's mother for making a typescript of Part 1 in 1965; both sets for their moral and financial support; Leon's father not so much for saying: "Never mind! We will soon feed you up!" when he saw Leon wheel his bike up the garden path at the end of the trip.

Also, posthumously we thank all our mentors over the years, amongst them especially Robin Pitman at Borlase; John thanks Ken Bayes at Design Research Unit for lessons in lateral thinking: Leon thanks Richard Hamilton at the University of Newcastle upon Tyne for lessons in analytical drawing.

Finally, we thank Stuart Geddes for his work on the book. To state that he designed it, which he did, is too glib. It suggests an aesthetic ordering, which it is, but it is also the surfacing of a logic from the texts and images that makes the book – we believe - so much more than the sum of its constituent parts.

ABOUT THE AUTHORS

Leon van Schaik AO is an emeritus professor of architecture at RMIT University.

John Turner is a British architect with worldwide experience on projects associated with the physical, mental, educational and social wellbeing of people. He lives in France.

TRIP 1964:
*in which a cycling trip to Rome is resurrected*
Leon van Schaik and John Turner

First published in 2022

This publication is copyrighted and all rights are reserved. Apart from any use as permitted under the *Copyright Act 1968*, no part may be reproduced or communicated to the public by any process without prior written permission. Enquiries should be directed to the authors.

© The authors

ISBN: 978-0-6484286-2-6

A catalogue record for this book is available from the National Library of Australia.

Copy editing by Annie Jermain
Designed and typeset by Stuart Geddes.
Printed by Ingram Spark

www.ingramcontent.com/pod-product-compliance
Lightning Source LLC
Chambersburg PA
CBHW041501010526
44107CB00049B/1609